Empathetic Communication

Type of Communication and Powerful Speakers

Copyright © 2022

All rights reserved.

The content contained within this book may not be reproduced, duplicated or transmitted without direct written permission from the author or the publisher.

Under no circumstances will any blame or legal responsibility be held against the publisher, or author, for any damages, reparation, or monetary loss due to the information contained within this book, either directly or indirectly.

Legal Notice:

This book is copyright protected. It is only for personal use. You cannot amend, distribute, sell, use, quote or paraphrase any part, or the content within this book, without the consent of the author or publisher.

Disclaimer Notice:

Please note the information contained within this document is for educational and entertainment purposes only. All effort has been executed to present accurate, up to date, reliable, complete information. No warranties of any kind are declared or implied. Readers acknowledge that the author is not engaged in the rendering of legal, financial, medical or professional advice. The content within this book has been derived from various sources.

By reading this document, the reader agrees that under no circumstances is the author responsible for any losses, direct or indirect, that are incurred as a result of the use of the information contained within this document, including, but not limited to, errors, omissions, or inaccuracies.

CONTENTS

Introduction
Chapter 1: The Importance of Effective Communication
Chapter 2: Types of Communication
Chapter 3: How to Build Emotional Connections
Chapter 4: Overcoming Speech Obstacles
Chapter 5: Indirectly Influencing Others
Chapter 6: Making Your Words Effective
Chapter 7: Practice Makes Perfect
Chapter 8: Managing Conflict
Chapter 9: Empathetic Communication
Chapter 10: Powerful Speakers Can Change the World
Conclusion

Introduction

Do you ever struggle to put your thoughts into words when communicating? Do you choke up when you have to speak up for yourself in difficult situations? Are you awkward once the small talk ends? These are all signs that you need to work toward having more effective communication. Being able to communicate effectively is a crucial skill to have in life, as it can help you to build relationships, improve your friendships, and further yourself in your career.

How do you know whether you're in need of learning effective communication skills? Maybe you find yourself avoiding social interactions, as you fear having to communicate with others, or you notice yourself completely freezing up in conversation. You might be the opposite, as you find yourself talking non-stop. Do you find that you have word vomit that makes you say things that you end up regretting? If you've related to any of these examples, then this is the perfect book for you.

Feeling stunted by your communication skills can be overwhelming, as you don't know how to get a conversation going. This not only impacts your relationships in life, but it also has a negative influence on your confidence and self-esteem. Not being able to start to engage in conversation can make you feel awkward and shy. This may be an insecurity of yours that people even comment on.

Your unhealthy and ineffective communication will become a thing of the past once you read through this book, as it will teach you how to communicate with confidence and style. You may have specific communication goals that you want to reach, and those can be achieved through this book. For example, you may have a speech to perform, but you need to improve your public speaking skills first. Or, you could be experiencing lots of conflict with a person close to you, as all of your communication turns into arguments.

You won't only learn how to communicate properly through speaking skills, but you'll also learn other valuable skills of communication. You'll learn how your body language plays a big role in how you communicate effectively. You will also develop better listening skills, which in return make you a better communicator. Another of the most valuable communication skills that you can take away from this book is being able to indirectly influence other people with your communication by using effective psychological tricks.

To learn all the fruitful and effective communication skills that have been mentioned, you need to continue reading this book with an open mind. Be open to learning how you can change and communicate better, and be prepared to make your anxiety, awkwardness, and ineffective communication a thing of the past!

CHAPTER 1

The Importance of Effective Communication

"Communication is a skill that you can learn. It's like riding a bicycle or typing. If you're willing to work at it, you can rapidly improve the quality of every part of your life." – Brian Tracy

When you think about communication, what makes it important for you? It may be its value of helping you express yourself, or it could be valuable for building new friendships. Communication can be seen differently for each person, so it's important for you to determine what it means to you. Once you understand what communication means to you, you can start to realize all the ways it is important in your life.

Without communication, we don't tell people how we feel, we can't be educated, and we can't create valuable relationships. This is what makes communication so valuable, as it makes our world go round. To understand each other in life, it's crucial to have effective communication that helps us verbalize what we think and feel. How you communicate has an impact on how you represent yourself to the world.

A World With Ineffective Communication

You may be thinking to yourself how important it is for you to work on communicating effectively. Do you really need to change your communication skills, and become better at engaging in conversations? The answer to these questions is yes, as communicating effectively makes a huge impact on your life, as well as the people around you. These are some examples of ineffective communication that you might be struggling with in your life:

- **Talking just to be heard.** When you have a conversation with someone, do you talk to respond to what the other person said, or are you focused on just speaking to be heard? Many people talk just to be heard, which causes them to neglect other people in the conversation. Doing this can find you in a position where the two of you are having different conversations, and no one is understanding the other.
- **Interrupting other people.** If you are someone who doesn't listen to other people, then you may find that you have an unhealthy habit of interrupting others. When you interrupt people frequently, you will get into the habit of doing it frequently. This means that you won't even be aware when you're guilty of doing it. Although you may do it unintentionally, it can end up offending the person you interrupt. When someone is trying to

communicate something to you, and you constantly interrupt them without trying to listen to them, it makes it appear as though you don't care about what they have to say. This can negatively impact your relationships in life, as well as cause more arguments and disputes.
- **Being unable to say what's on your mind.** You may find that your way of communicating negatively impacts your ability to stand up for yourself. When you find yourself in situations where you feel uncomfortable, upset, and unheard, you may struggle to find the confidence to stand up for yourself. In life it's so important to stand up for yourself when you need to, or else you will find yourself being taken advantage of by the people around you.
- **Speaking with no filter.** At the other end of the spectrum, you may find that you have verbal diarrhea, which causes you to talk endlessly without thinking before you speak.

Doing this can be dangerous, as you end up saying hurtful and mean things that you regret later. Although it's important to say what's on your mind, you still need to consider other people's feelings. If you're someone who speaks with no filter, you've probably upset someone, experienced misunderstandings, and ruined relationships with your ineffective communication.

- **Avoiding socializing.** Do you have so much anxiety and fear about communicating that you avoid socializing by all means? You may find that social interactions and communicating are too much for you mentally, so you choose to avoid them altogether. This approach to life can make you miss out on many opportunities that could be good for you. For example, you avoid making new friendships, or pursuing romantic relationships that could benefit your life. You also may doubt your confidence when it comes to your professional life, which can make you miss out on various opportunities.

Consider how your ineffective communication may be negatively impacting your life. We often don't realize how crucial good communication is, as we fail to recognize the problems ineffective communication causes. If you identified with any of the above examples in any way, then this is the right book for you.

In each chapter you will learn new ways to improve your communication, which will eliminate any of the issues you experience from your unhealthy communication patterns. It's important to realize where and how you are communicating wrongly so that you can find ways to improve your conversations.

What Is Effective Communication?

Now that you have a good understanding of what ineffective communication is, it's important for you to learn the type of communication you should be using. Having effective communication skills can help you to get a message across in a clear, concise, and respectful manner.

You're able to voice concerns, stand up for yourself and your opinions, as well as attentively listen to others with empathy, all while maintaining respect and understanding for the people you talk to. Throughout this book, we will show you effective communication practices that will make you speak with purpose and clarity.

Understanding Conversations

If you want to understand the importance of effective communication, you need to be able to understand conversations, and why they add value to our lives. Understanding the ins and outs of conversations is the first step to the journey toward effective and efficient communication. Some of us have hundreds of conversations in a day, whereas others just have a few. The amount of conversation you have in a day doesn't matter when your conversations are valuable and effective.

What is a Conversation?

When you see this question, you may think the answer is quite obvious. A conversation is when two people engage in dialogue for various topics and occasions. But, to truly understand what a conversation is, we need to take a deeper look at it instead of focusing on surface value. Considering the different factors that make a conversation what it is can help you understand why they're so valuable. These are some qualities that make a conversation:

- **Listening to each other.** Having a conversation isn't just talking to each other, as it's a two-way road. If you want to have an effective and healthy conversation, both parties need to be open to listening actively. You need to hear what each person has to say before you find ways to reply. Listening to each other also helps to build context, which essentially allows you to understand what the other person is trying to say, and how you can answer them properly.

- **Speaking your mind.** When you have a conversation, you are talking about what you're thinking. A conversation is essentially swapping mental thoughts verbally. This makes it important for you to consider what you're thinking before you speak. Give people your honest opinion that aligns with your thoughts, but while doing this you must learn how to filter your thoughts. You can't always say exactly what you think, as it may come out offensive and hurtful.
- **Building relationships.** To build a relationship in your life—whether

it's a friendship, romantic relationship, or work relationship—you need to be able to communicate to grow your bond. With every conversation you have together, you learn more about each other, and your relationship becomes closer. This is how conversations are used to bring people together, as it's a way to comfort, make jokes, and understand each other.

Many people don't engage in conversations as they should. Conversations are valuable moments of dialogue that help you to get a better understanding of others and their thoughts. Having healthy and effective conversations can make life easier and more enjoyable, as you not only learn more about the people around you, but you're also able to help others understand you more! Some other elements of conversations you should consider include:

- **Asking.** This is when you seek information from another person

during your conversation. We all ask questions at times in conversation to show our interest, and learn more about the topics of conversations.
- **Proposing.** You are putting forward an idea that you believe in. You may have to convince someone of something you want, so you propose this idea to them in the best way possible, through healthy communication.
- **Attacking.** On the other hand, a conversation can include attacking, as you or the other person doesn't appreciate the proposed idea. When attacking occurs in a conversation, it often turns into an argument.
- **Excluding and including.** A conversation doesn't only have to occur between two people, as others can get involved. How you communicate with the other people around you shows them whether you're being inclusive or exclusive. It's valuable to include others in conversations to make them feel heard and seen.

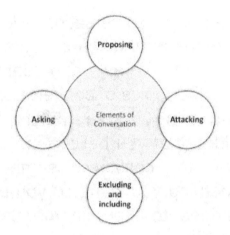

Types of Conversations

To understand what conversations truly are, it's valuable to consider the different types of conversations you can engage in. You will have countless conversations in your lifetime, so you are bound to encounter these four different types of conversations at some point:

- **Debate.** A debate is a two-way conversation, where both parties have an objective and a motive they are discussing. The goal of the conversation is for one person to persuade the other person into agreeing with their point of view, so the former can win the argument. For example, you and your partner have to make an important life decision, but you have opposing ideas for dealing with the situation. You can have a debate to persuade each other, and ultimately make a unanimous decision together.

- **Dialogue.** A dialogue is also a two-way conversation that most of us engage in frequently throughout the day. This is when you exchange information with another person through discussion. Dialogue is used in our daily lives to help us learn about others, as well as build relationships with them. You can see examples of dialogue through your everyday life, as you have dialogues with customers, family members, and your friends.
- **Discourse.** Discourse is different from the other types of conversations, as it's a one-way conversation. It's when one person delivers information, either in the

form of the spoken or written word. For example, when a professor gathers students to discuss a book they're studying, the professor will be the only one delivering information.

- **Diatribe.** Diatribe is also a one-way conversation, but its objective is much like the goal of debating. When you diatribe, you are the only one speaking, trying to convince or persuade someone else. This form of conversation may also be used to express to someone how you're feeling. For example, if you are having a fight with a friend, you take a moment to discuss how you feel, and persuade them to understand your perspective without disruptions.

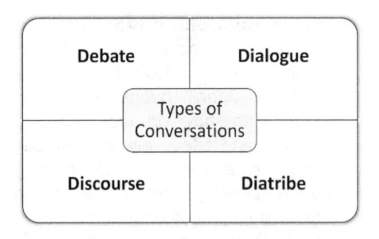

Why Effective Conversations Are Important

When you consider why conversations are important to you, you may think of a very brief response that pops in your head first. However, conversations serve so much purpose in our lives without us even recognizing it. There are various reasons why conversations are valuable, and need to be practiced frequently in life. These are just a few reasons why conversations are so important:

- **Fixing miscommunications.** As life becomes more fast-paced, our communication follows in its footsteps. Many people have lost touch with how to communicate healthily and effectively, as they say things in a rush without thinking before speaking. This is what makes effective conversations so important, as they help you fix miscommunications. Not only does effective communication help you to clear up miscommunications, but it can also help you to avoid having these miscommunications in the first place.
- **Avoiding conflict.** Words are the number one starter for conflict, as misunderstandings and hurtful words can upset any person. When you have effective conversations, it helps to avoid conflict in various ways. Avoiding miscommunications can prevent conflict occurring from these misunderstandings. You will also find that having a healthy conversation during conflict by listening to each

other attentively helps you resolve many of your problems.

- **Understanding each other.** How well do you know the people in your life? You may think you know every detail of the people in your life, but there's so much you can learn through healthy conversations. When you have conversations with the people you know ,or even complete strangers, you learn a lot about them, and they also learn about you. You are able to communicate your boundaries, so people know how to treat you. Your conversations can let people know how you're feeling and what you're thinking, so they can understand why you behave the way you do.

Traits of a Confident Communicator

When you think of your communication style, would you consider yourself a confident communicator or not? You may think that you are a confident and assertive communicator, but when it comes down to having conversations, maybe you don't say things in the way you hoped.

Being a successful communicator is all about approaching conversations with confidence in yourself. Being a confident communicator helps you to build the best, healthiest relationship. It can also help you in your career, as you communicate with people professionally with no self-doubt. These are some traits that can help you to become someone who communicates with confidence:

- **Empathetic.** People who are confident communicators are able to be empathetic toward the people they communicate with. This means that they actively listen to what other people have to say, as they are sensitive to their needs. When people use empathy to listen to others, they actually take into consideration what they have to say, and they reply accordingly. This can

influence genuine conversations that leave both parties happy.
- **Sincerity.** Being sincere when communicating is an essential trait confident communicators have. They leave the sarcasm and passive aggression behind, so their communication sounds sincere and genuine to the other parties. Not only do they communicate sincerely, but they ensure that everything they say is honest. They are not afraid to tell the truth, no matter how difficult it may be to communicate.
- **Assertive.** Confident communicators are able to stand up for themselves when they need to. If they want someone to know how they feel, or they need someone to do a task for them, they can communicate this assertively. This helps others to understand what your boundaries and requests are for their relationship with you. Being assertive in life is often necessary, so you don't get walked over.

- **Respectful.** Although confident communicators are assertive with what they want, they also find a way to communicate what they want in a respectful manner. You want other people to respect you, not fear you, and this can be accomplished by respecting them first. Whatever you have on your mind that you want to communicate, you need to ensure that you use a balance of assertiveness and respect.

Benefits of Understanding Conversations

You may be wondering how understanding conversations can be beneficial for your journey toward communicating effectively. When you understand the basics and importance of conversations, you will be able to use conversations as the building blocks for your effective communication.

Knowing how important conversations are in our everyday lives will help you to utilize them correctly. When you understand how to use conversations to improve your confidence, relationships, and career, you will discover how powerful and important effective communication truly is!

CHAPTER 2

Types of Communication

"Although we live in an information technology age, we often find ourselves in failure to communicate situations." – Johnny Tan

As there are types of conversations, there are also types of communication that impact how effectively you communicate with others. If you want to build those relationships, restore your confidence, positively influence the people around you, and become the best version of yourself, you need to explore the different forms of communication you can practice.

Four Types of Communication

When you're communicating, you don't necessarily take the time to consider what type of communication you're practicing, but knowing this information can be beneficial for your journey toward effective communication. There are various ways people choose to communicate, and these different forms determine how well you communicate with others. The following are merely four types of communication that have an impact on how you converse with others.

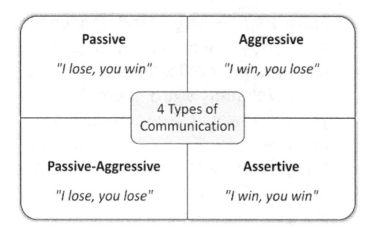

Passive

If you are at the more shy and soft-spoken end of the spectrum of communication, you fall under this category. Being passive means that you shy away from speaking your mind or objecting to something you don't believe in. Passive communicators want to avoid conflict at all costs, so they choose to keep their opinions to themselves, rather than starting conflict. These are some signs that you're a passive communicator:

- **Inability to say "No".** You've had a long day at work and your boss calls you after office hours to do some voluntary extra hours. He asks you if you would like to participate because they really need help. You really don't want to do it, but you're afraid to disappoint him, so you just say yes. If a similar scenario has happened to you, you may be a passive communicator. People who are more passive in conversations struggle to say "no" to others, even when they really want to.

- **Avoiding eye contact.** Passive communicators are usually less confident in themselves when they speak. They often don't believe in what they're saying, and their ability to communicate it properly. This usually causes them to avoid eye contact when talking, especially when they talk about something they feel less confident in, which makes them feel awkward.
- **"I lose, you win."** Using passive communication is a "I lose, you win" sort of situation. When you use a passive approach to communication, you're essentially going with the flow, which means you don't stand up for yourself and what you believe in. This can cause you to be in situations where you're getting the short end of the stick, and the other person gets exactly what they want.

Aggressive

On the other side of the spectrum, you could be using aggressive communication. This type of communication is the opposite of the passive approach, as it's forceful, rude, and intimidating. When you are approached with aggressive communication, you can feel it. These are some signs you are using aggressive communication:

- **Being overly critical and rude.** Aggressive communicators often express what's on their mind in a rude and critical way. They can get worked up and say really hurtful things that upset the other person. For example, if something bad happens, they can say something like, "It's all your fault." These hurtful words end up making the other person feel guilty and in the wrong.
- **Commanding others.** People who use a more aggressive approach toward communicating have the tendency to command others around them. If you neglect other people's feelings, and fail to

listen to them because you want things your way, it's a sign that you're an aggressive communicator. This can make you a more commanding person, who intimidates other people into doing things their way.
- **"I win, you lose."** Unlike passive communication, aggressive communication leaves you winning, and the other person loses. You are so commanding and rigid that you only allow for things to go your way. You neglect other people's thoughts and feelings, which leaves them at the losing end of the situation. You may benefit from the situation, but this is done in an unfair manner that negatively impacts the relationships in your life.

Passive-Aggressive

Passive-aggressive communication is one of the worst types, as it can be manipulative and hurtful. On a surface level it may seem like someone is being passive to you, but there are deeper reasons behind their words that have harsh intent. Passive-aggressive communicators use their words in discrete and subtle ways to guilt or manipulate you into letting them get their way. These are some signs that you're a passive-aggressive communicator:

- **Being in denial.** Many people who are guilty of using passive aggressive communication aren't able to admit that they do. They often feel powerless and frustrated in negative situations, and they don't know how to communicate it effectively. Even though they use toxic tactics that can be hurtful for the other party, they struggle to admit to themselves that they're being passive aggressive.
- **Using silent treatment.** Instead of openly communicating their problems, passive-aggressive communicators use the silent treatment as a tactic to get what they want. To make the other party feel guilty or bad for going against them

in a situation, they will use silent treatment to get back at them. This is an unhealthy tactic that doesn't help you to deal with situations in the best way.
- **"I lose, you lose."** The reason why this is the worst communication type is because everyone loses. When you use passive aggression to get what you want, not only do you lose in the situation, but so does the other person. You end up feeling sorry for yourself, and using toxic tactics that only upset you more. The other party also ends up losing in the situation, as they start to feel guilty.

Assertive

Ultimately, this is the type of communication you should be aiming to use on a consistent basis. Being assertive is a healthy and confident way to communicate, as you stand up for yourself while still respecting other people around you. These are some signs that you're an assertive communicator:

- **Using 'I' statements.** When you communicate assertively, you become more confident in representing yourself and your thoughts. This helps you to use "I" in statements standing up for yourself, which shows other people what you're feeling and thinking. Being able to confidently express your thoughts also convinces others more.
- **Listening to others.** When you communicate assertively, you not only communicate your side of the story with confidence, but you also listen attentively to the other person's perspective. This helps you to understand what the other person is thinking and feeling, which allows you to come up with a more informed and healthy response.
- **"I win, you win."** This is what makes being assertive the best communication style. When you are assertive to the people you're

communicating with, you don't forcefully command them to choose your side of the situation. This means that you win, as you get your point across, and may even end up persuading other people into taking your side. The other party also wins in this situation, as they start to understand where you're coming from, which can help them to choose your side of the situation.

Other Forms of Communication

These four types of communication aren't the only ones out there, as there are other forms to consider. These other forms of communication that help you understand what the tone and mood of a conversation is. It's valuable to know when to use these different forms of communication in your everyday life.

Different situations in life require different communication styles, and it's valuable to choose the appropriate communication style for your specific situation. These are a few other forms of communication, and examples of when you should use them in life:

- **Formal communication.** We've all experienced a moment where we had to engage in formal conversation. When you're in a formal setting such as your office, you need to be able to talk with respect and formality. It's important to know when it's required of you to communicate formally, so you can talk appropriately in a formal setting. For example, you may get into a work dispute that requires you to go to a hearing. In this situation you can't speak casually and use slang, as it will negatively reflect on your professionalism. You need to be able to talk formally, and state your case in a respectful manner.
- **Informal communication.** On the other hand, there are also situations where informal communication is necessary. If you

constantly walk around using formal communication, you'll never be able to have relationship-building conversations. We use informal communication more often throughout our days, as it brings us closer to the people around us. For example, if you have to speak to someone empathetically because they are going through something difficult in their life, you need to use more informal and casual language. If you try to comfort some with formal language, you may find that you end up sounding cold and insincere. Using more informal language can help you express compassion to the best of your ability.

- **Non-verbal communication.** Communication doesn't always have to be expressed verbally, as there are many other ways we communicate with each other, sometimes without even realizing it. We don't only communicate with our mouths, but we also communicate with our expressions, postures, and gestures. Using non-verbal communication is valuable in situations where you can't verbally communicate, as your face and body can tell people a lot about what you're thinking and feeling. For example, if you find yourself in an uncomfortable position where someone won't leave you alone, you can use your body language and facial expressions to show your discomfort. As the other person notices your non-verbal communication, they get the message that you want to be left alone.

- **Written communication.** On the note of non-verbal communication, written communication is a type that you could consider at times. If you're not someone who uses their body language to express how they feel, and you don't know how to tell someone something verbally, then written communication may be the right fit for your situation. Using written communication helps you to say exactly what you're thinking, especially if you're feeling nervous. For example, you want to tell someone you have romantic feelings for them, but you're too nervous to do it verbally. Every time you try you stutter and fail and express how you feel. You can write a nice romantic letter that shows the other person exactly how you feel.

Which Type Do You Use?

After considering the four different types of communication, you should consider which type you use the most. Discovering this information will help you to determine whether you're using effective communication or not. These are some tips that will help you to discover what type of communication you use, and whether it's effective:

- **Self-reflection.** To determine what type of communication you use, you need to be able to do some self-reflection. You need to reflect on the ways you communicate, so you can determine what types of conversations you're having. Think about the last few conversations you've had, especially when you were in conflict with someone. How did you communicate? Were you passive or assertive in the situation?

- **Be honest with yourself.** Consider your communication style and be honest with how effective or ineffective it may be. You may discover that you have an unhealthy communication style that has been negatively impacting the relationships in your life. Discovering that your communication type is aggressive or passive-aggressive can be difficult to come to terms with. To work on your ineffective communication techniques, you need to be aware of your unhealthy habits you have.
- **Ask the people in your life.** To determine what type of communication you use in conflict,

ask the people you've had conflict with. They will be able to tell you from first-hand experience how you communicate when a situation is tense. This helps you to hear from the people in your life how you made them feel through your communication. If they tell you that they've been hurt by your type of communication before, as you are too aggressive or passive-aggressive, then it's important to take accountability for your words. Let them know that you acknowledge where you went wrong, and promise to improve your communication type during conflict.

Determining what your communication type is can help you to understand whether you need to improve it, as well as you can learn how to accomplish this. It can make you aware of unhealthy communication habits you've been guilty of in your conversations. This can help you to avoid being aggressive, passive-aggressive, or passive when communicating with the people in your life.

Your objective should be to achieve assertive communication, as it will help you to get your perspective across in a confident and respectful manner. Assertive communication is the best style of communication to use, especially when you find yourself in conflict with someone. Being assertive with your communication also gets you better results, as people listen to you when you speak with confidence and assurance in yourself. These are some tips that can help you become a more assertive communicator:

- **Take ownership.** To be an assertive communicator, you need to be able to take ownership of your thoughts and actions. When you communicate something, you should make it apparent that you take full ownership and believe in your opinion and what you're saying. To take ownership of what you say, utilize 'I,' maintain eye contact, and say what you mean with conviction.

- **Say "no" sometimes.** Being assertive means that you avoid being a pushover. When you're confronted by a situation you don't want to be a part of, instead of blindly agreeing, you acknowledge when you need to say "no." You need to learn how to say no, even when you know it's going to disappoint someone. There are times in life where you just need to prioritize yourself and your best interests.
- **Speak up for yourself.** Assertive communication requires you to speak up for yourself when necessary. If you are feeling upset, uncomfortable, or anxious about something, you need to build up the confidence to speak up for yourself. For example, if someone says something rude to you and it offends you, you need to stand up for yourself by telling this person you didn't appreciate it. Speaking up for yourself helps you to get more respect from the people in your life.

CHAPTER 3

How to Build Emotional Connections

"Verbal communication is essential in order to understand what is going on inside other people. If they do not tell us their thoughts, their feelings, and their experiences, we are left to guess." –Dr. Gary Chapman

You may be interested in improving your communication skills to build emotional connections. We all want to have close relationships that add value and happiness to our lives. This makes it crucial to use your communication to build healthy relationships and emotional connections. The power of words and conversations is what truly creates emotional connections. All you need to learn is how to use conversations and communication styles to your advantage!

The First Impression

When you are forming new relationships in your life, the first impression means everything! When we meet people for the first time, we form a perception about them from our experience with them. You may claim that you don't judge and assume things about people when you first meet them, but it's almost human nature for us to gather first impressions from people we meet for the first time. This is how you can make a good first impression to people you meet for the first time:

- **Smile and use eye contact.** When people talk to you, their main focus is going to be on your face. This means you should try your best to use it to show the right expression and eye contact that show warmth and friendliness. Smiling every now

and then when it's appropriate during the conversation shows people how much you're interested in talking to them. Maintaining eye contact frequently also shows that you're a confident communicator, which makes the conversation feel more personal and attentive.
- **Positive body language.** Believe it or not, but people observe your body language when they're communicating with you. The body language you use makes an impression on the other person, as they may subconsciously or consciously observe how you are toward them. For example, if you have your arms crossed and your body turned away from them, it may make them think that you're not interested in talking to them. This may leave them with a negative impression of you, so be sure to use open and positive body language as you communicate.
- **Be authentic.** You want your first impression to be a positive one that

really reflects who you are as an individual. This means that you should be your authentic self when you first meet someone. You may want to put your best foot forward and show them the best version of yourself that doesn't truly reflect you, but doing this only gives other people a false perception of who you are. They will have an unrealistic impression that you can't recreate when you see them again. Being authentic and honest gives other people the chance to connect with the real you, which can improve how they see you.

- **Don't try too hard.** When you are trying to get a good first impression, there's a lot of different things you can consider to communicate in the best way possible. However, it's also important to find a balance, as you don't want to find yourself trying too hard. When you try too hard it can give you a bad impression, as you seem like a try-hard who isn't sincere. You need to put in an effort, but don't force people to have a good impression of you, as they will come up with their own assumptions.

How to Build a Good First Impression With Dialogue

Learning how to communicate effectively with a complete stranger can be a bit overwhelming. You have no idea how to relate to each other, or how to communicate with each other yet. However, how you communicate when you first meet a stranger can set the tone for the rest of your relationship, so you need to ensure that you make a good first impression with your dialogue. Below is an example of how you can use dialogue to make a good impression.

You: *Hi, my name is (insert your name). I could see you have great energy, so I'd love to get to know you better. What's your name?*

Stranger: *That's so nice. I'm Maxine.*

You: *This is my first time coming to this yoga class. I've only joined because I really need to get into better shape. I literally lose my breath from walking to my kitchen, haha. What brings you to yoga?*

Stranger: *Haha, similar reason. I just feel like yoga is the best form of exercise that keeps me grounded. You should come here more often, I've been coming for months! I could use a yoga friend.*

You: *That sounds perfect. I'll see you again next week, Maxine!*

This example is a great way to create a good first impression. You made the first move by trying to form a friendship in your new yoga class. You were authentic, and showed your sense of humor, which made the stranger warm up to you. She even offered to become your yoga friend. By asking her about herself, and not talking too much about yourself, you showed Maxine that you are someone who could be a great, attentive friend.

Building a Healthy Relationship

When you are trying to nurture an emotional connection and build a healthy relationship, there are various things you should consider. You want to use your healthy and effective communication to open up to the people around you, so it can help you to build new relationships, as well as restore old ones. To build a healthy relationship and an emotional connection with someone, you should focus on using your effective communication to build trust and rapport.

Building Trust

Another important part of building emotional connections is being able to build trust with people. The foundation of a healthy relationship is trust, so it's important for you to build that trust through your communication. Building trust is all about being a reliable and friendly individual whom people want to have around in their lives. These are some tips that will help you to build trust with your new relationships and emotional connections:

- When you want to build strong emotional relationships, you need to remember that effective communication is key. You need to be able to have healthy conversations where you both **actively listen to each other, and respond accordingly**. When you have miscommunications, they can often lead to unnecessary conflict and arguments that dampen the trust in your new relationship.
- The best way emotional connections are built is when the other person can see how much you care about them in negative situations. You want to be a person that they can confide in during challenging times. When these individuals communicate with you about their negative circumstances and open up to you, it's important for you to *express*

your compassion and care for their situation. This will show them that you're a trusting person who has their best interest at heart.
- When trying to build trust, not only should you allow a safe space for the other person to open up, but you should ***try to open up to them as well***. Being open to the people around you encourages them to do the same, as well as shows them your sincerity. If you are trying to be open with someone, you should have moments where you become vulnerable. This means you show them a side of you when you're upset or overwhelmed; this helps them see you as a more relatable person they can comfort. It's also important to be honest and transparent when building a relationship, so you can show this person that you have nothing to hide. This builds trust, as they know you're not lying or hiding anything from them.

Building Rapport

Another way you can work on building a healthy relationship is by building rapport between you and the other individual. Rapport is a sense of connection you develop when you build a relationship with someone you like and trust. When you build rapport, you develop a bond with the other person, as you share the same interests, priorities, and mindset. Building rapport in a newly found relationship can help you grow a genuine connection, as you both find genuine interest in getting to know and understand each other more. These are some steps that can help you to develop rapport between you and a new life relationship, and emotional connection that you're pursuing:

1. **Find common ground.** If you're trying to build rapport with someone, you want to find ways in which you can relate with each other. This makes it valuable for you to determine what common ground you

share. Finding common interests and life experiences can help you to connect on a deeper level. You can have conversations about this common ground, and this can influence even more communication and moments of bonding.
2. **Create shared experiences.** Another way to form a bond with someone is by creating shared experiences together. If you have similar interests or hobbies that you enjoy, you can engage in them together. This creates a positive experience that you can remember and bond over, which will strengthen your relationship. If you find that you don't have much in common, you can create new experiences together that can bring you closer. These experiences become a topic of discussion, and moments of bonding, that you'll remember for a long time.
3. **Restrain judgment.** When you're working on building a new relationship with rapport, you need to reserve your judgments. It can be

human instinct for us to judge others at times, but it's important to prevent yourself from indulging in this unhealthy habit. Judging people when you meet them can influence how you communicate with them. People want to build relationships where they feel comfortable to be open and vulnerable. When you judge them and say judgemental things, you can ruin this growing bond, as they start to think you aren't a safe space.

Asking Questions

A big part of forming healthy relationships is being able to ask the right questions, as well as answer other people's questions. Questions are a lot more valuable for effective communication than you may realize. Asking the right questions in conversations helps you to learn a lot about others, which can help to build healthy and happy relationships.

The Importance of Asking the Right Questions

Questions can be a valuable communication tool when you use them correctly. There are many benefits you can receive from asking questions throughout your improved communication journey. Being able to ask the right questions at the right moment can help you to build a relationship in many ways. Here are some important aspects of asking the right questions:

- **Showing interest.** When you ask questions in conversation with someone, it shows that you're interested in what they have to say. Asking them the right questions that are in context with what they're talking about makes them feel like you are listening attentively to what they're saying. From your questions, they know that you are genuinely interested in what they have to say, which gives them a positive impression of you. This strengthens a relationship, as it shows your ability to care about others.

- **Breaking the ice.** Talking to someone you don't know very well can be extremely awkward at times. You may find yourself struggling with awkward silences, as you're unsure of what you should talk about with each other. You've run out of all of your small talk, as you've spoken about the weather twice already. Asking questions can be an effective way to break the ice, as you start conversations with interesting questions. When you break the ice with these questions, you will find that you both get more comfortable to talk normally.
- **Learning more.** Asking the right questions can also help you discover more about the other person. When you first meet someone, or you're building a new relationship, there's so much you can learn about them. This makes it so valuable to ask questions to discover this information. These questions can

help you to understand who they are as individuals, why they do things and say the things they do, and how they would like to be treated within your relationship.

- **Understanding without jumping to conclusions.** Often relationships start on the wrong foot, as assumptions are made. When you meet someone you may assume something negative about them, which can start conflict, damaging the fragile stage of your relationship-building. This can all be avoided by asking the right questions. When you ask questions instead of assuming, you find out the truth about others. It also makes people feel heard and loved when you ask questions instead of assuming things automatically.

Examples of Questions to Ask

If you're struggling to find questions you can use to break the ice in a conversation, discover more about someone, or search for more clarity, these examples can help you. There are various types of questions you can ask in different conversations. You just need to determine what questions are applicable at that moment.

Example 1 - Initiating Conversation

For this dialogue example, you can see how questions can be used to break the ice, and initiate effective communication with a stranger.

Stranger: *What work do you do?*

You: *I'm a baker. I have my own businesses, and I make everything from cakes and cupcakes to savory treats.*

You: *I heard that you are into engineering? Is this just an interest or is it your profession?*

Stranger: *It's actually both my interest and my profession.*

You: *That's so interesting. Please tell me more about what you do!*

In this example you can see how you can initiate a more in-depth conversation with follow-up questions, instead of simply asking what the other person's job is and stopping. By showing genuine interest in this person's passion, you learn a lot more about them than just their occupation. In this example you can also see how you don't steal the limelight by talking about yourself. You answer their question, but you turn the conversation back to them.

Example 2 - Resolving Conflict

This example shows you how you can use questions to resolve conflict or tension you feel with someone in your life.

Your spouse: *Are you upset with me now?*

You: *I'm feeling a little bit hurt, but I want to clear up the situation. Why did you choose to decline all of my calls yesterday?*

Your spouse: *I'm very sorry that I did, but I was extremely busy throughout the day. My boss was extremely demanding, and I didn't even have time to talk to you.*

You: *I understand. Maybe in the future you can send me a message or call me telling me you're very busy, so I don't jump to conclusions.*

Your spouse: *Of course, I can do that for you. Thank you for understanding, babe.*

In this example, conflict is resolved speedily, before any argument can break loose. It's extremely important to ask the people in your life about situations before jumping to conclusions. In this scenario, you could've jumped to conclusions and accused your partner of cheating on you, and this would turn into a bigger argument. By asking questions and hearing reasonings behind the situation, you can find closure and resolution.

How to Use Questions Effectively

Believe it or not, but there is a right and wrong way to use questions. If you abuse asking questions, you will find the results to be ineffective. You want to find the right questions to ask, as well as the right way to ask them. Doing this will help you to appear curious and interested, but not overbearing and rude. These following steps will help you to ask questions effectively:

1. **Ask at the right time.** As effective and valuable asking questions is, there are still some moments where using questions may not be appropriate. Before you ask the question you're thinking of, you need to consider if it's the appropriate time for a question. If your question is related to what the

other person is talking about, it's appropriate for that moment. You also need to strongly consider the atmosphere, as it may be a very serious conversation, where questions won't be entirely appreciated.
2. **Avoid asking personal questions.** When you're thinking of questions to ask, you need to avoid overly personal questions. You may be an open person who doesn't mind talking about private matters, but the person you're speaking to may not be as comfortable with this. You don't want to cross a boundary that makes them feel uncomfortable during your conversation. However, if this person you're talking to shows you that they like to talk about personal and private matters in their life, you can proceed to ask them questions about those.
3. **Don't overask.** Although it's important to ask questions when you're curious about something, you must also avoid asking too many

questions. Constantly asking someone question after question can make them feel overwhelmed. When you overwhelm someone with so many questions, it can make them frustrated. It can make them feel like they don't get the opportunity to talk properly without you interrupting, as well as make them feel as though they are being interrogated. It's important to find a healthy balance that shows your interest, but doesn't overwhelm who you're talking to.

4. **Word your questions nicely.** How you ask your questions has a strong influence on how well it's received. You may have good intentions when asking your questions, but the way you word it sounds offensive. This makes it crucial to think about what you're going to ask before you speak. Many people ask questions in an intimidating and condescending manner, without even realizing it, which negatively impacts their communication. For example, you

may be thinking you want to ask your new friend whether they're in a relationship or not, but when you ask you say, "So do you have a boyfriend, or are you just alone?" Although your intentions were good with this question, it may appear judgmental and rude to the other person, especially if they aren't in a relationship.

Different Types of Questions

There are various types of questions that can be used for different occasions. The type of questions you ask can make an impact on the type of knowledge or feedback you receive. It's beneficial to consider these different types of questions so you know how to word your questions suitably for specific situations. These are a few different types of questions:

- **Open and closed questions.** Any question that is intended to be answered is either an open or closed question. A closed question can only have two possible responses, which are usually in the form of "yes" or "no", and "true" and "false." For example, if you're asked whether you've eaten today, you can just answer "yes" or "no." An open question, however, allows more to be discussed in an answer. These types of questions instigate lengthier answers that can create discussions. For example, if you're asked what your favorite food is and why, you can have a more descriptive and thoughtful response.
- **Funnel questions.** Funnel questions differ from other forms of questions, as they aren't singular questions, but rather a set of questions related to each other. Using funnel questions helps you to find multiple answers so that you can understand the bigger picture. For example, if you are asking questions

about a situation that happened, you will start off by asking about what happened, and then proceed to ask follow-up questions. When you use funnel questions, you must be sure not to overask, so you don't interrogate the other person.
- **Leading questions.** If you want to ask a question that leads the other person to a specific answer, you're going to want to use a leading question. To ask a leading question, you need to word it in a way that makes the other person realize what you're thinking is a good idea. For example, you may ask, "Don't you enjoy spending time with me? " This question is worded in a way to persuade the other person to admit they are enjoying time with you. This type of question you need to use sparingly, as it can appear manipulative if you abuse it.
- **Rhetorical questions.** Rhetorical questions don't require a response, as they are used to make a point. This type of question is used to

persuade others, instead of getting an answer. It can be a little awkward to use rhetorical questions in everyday conversations, as the other person may not know whether they should answer it or not. However, if you word it smartly, and say it with the right tone, it will serve its purpose effectively. Rhetorical questions are usually utilized in speeches, as it helps you to make a statement.

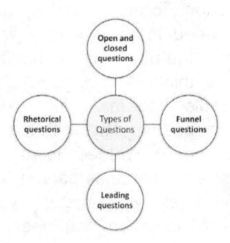

Give the Right Answers

Questions aren't only used for you to learn and understand more about other people, but they are also used as a way for other people to learn more about you. When you're having a conversation with someone new, they are bound to ask you some questions as well, to discover more about you. Learning how to answer questions politely, honestly, and to the point can help make a conversation run smoother.

How to Answer Questions Effectively

You may be thinking to yourself that answering questions is pretty straightforward and simple, but how you answer your questions can make a big impact on the effectiveness of your communication. Have you been answering questions in the wrong way this whole time? There's no wrong way to answer questions when you're answering honestly and openly, but there are some tips that can help you to find the best answers on the spot.

- When you get asked a question, it can be easy to get caught up in the moment by answering the first thing that pops into your mind. However, the best way to answer a question is by **thinking first before you speak**. When you feel put on the spot and you respond immediately, you may find your answer isn't what you want it to be. Although you may be fearful of having an awkward silence, it's valuable to pause before answering someone's question.
- If you feel confused or stumped by the question you've been asked, don't freeze up in fear. You can use this as an opportunity to **ask your own questions**. When a question is too difficult or confusing to answer, ask this person more questions about what they're trying to ask. In return, they will provide you with more clarity about the question, which will help you to answer the question confidently and honestly.
- If your objective is to build an emotional connection or healthy relationship, you need to be able to

transition your answers into casual conversation. You don't want the whole course of communication to be a relay of questions and answers between each other. This makes it valuable for you to find ways to branch out from your answer with your own statements, thoughts, or opinions. Doing this will also help the other person to talk more casually, and you will end up having a productive conversation.

- Conversations shouldn't be focused all on you, especially when you're working on building a relationship. Although you need to put effort into your answers and let the other person know all about you, you also don't want to take advantage of the opportunity by talking about yourself the whole time. This is why it's so important for you to **turn the conversation back to them** after answering a few questions. You can do this by asking them the same questions in return, or you could ask them completely different ones.

How to Handle Overwhelming Questions

You may find yourself struggling to answer someone's questions because they're a little too overwhelming for you. They may be invasive and inappropriate, which makes you uncomfortable. Or, the question is unanswerable and confusing, but when you ask for clarity, they don't provide you with it. Even though you may be working on communicating more effectively, the people that you may be talking to may not be the best at communication. So, it's important to prepare yourself for awkward and uncomfortable questions so you handle it in the best way possible. This is how you can handle overwhelming questions:

When you find the other person focusing on a topic that makes you feel uncomfortable, you can work on changing the direction of the conversation to something more appropriate. Just because the question was asked, and you want to impress this new person in your life, doesn't mean you're obliged to answer. Find a polite and respectful way to change the topic of conversation. You can use the bridging technique to change a topic seamlessly. This is an example of how you can diffuse this topic, and change it to something you're more comfortable with.

Friend: *How much money do you make every month?*

You: *Actually on that topic, I've been meaning to talk to HR about our paychecks, because the men in my office with the same job role as me are earning more! Can you believe that in this day and age men are still earning more than women?*

Friend: *That is horrible. I really hope you get that resolved. I actually saw a similar story about the gender pay gap in the sports industry.*

You: *Really? What did the story say?*

You have now diverted the conversation to a completely different topic. In this scenario, you weren't comfortable disclosing how much money you make to your friend, so thinking of something relative to this topic helped you to divert the conversation. You can now discuss something you're more comfortable with.

If you're really stumped and you have no idea what the other person is trying to ask you, you can use the old trick of answering a question with a question. You can ask them why they asked the question, and why the answer is important to them. Asking more details about their question and why they asked it may make them realize how inappropriate it is, which can help you both to move onto another topic.

Feeling uncomfortable with a question can make you react emotionally. You may misinterpret a question, and find yourself getting really offended by it. Although you are entitled to your own emotions, you need to find healthy ways to react to these uncomfortable questions. Calmly respond to the question with a short and sweet answer. Avoid saying anything hurtful and irrational that you may regret later.

CHAPTER 4

Overcoming Speech Obstacles

"There is no communication that is so simple that it cannot be misunderstood."
– Luigina Sgarro

You may be prepared to utilize effective communication, but as soon as you try you are met with speech obstacles. Many of us experience speech obstacles that cause us to communicate with others ineffectively. Do you find yourself getting fearful or anxious when you communicate, which causes you to stumble on your words? Struggling to be in control of your communication can be challenging when you're faced with obstacles.

You may not even be aware of your communication issues that act as stumbling blocks throughout your effective communication journey. It's quite important to take some time to be aware of mannerisms and speech obstacles that are holding you back in life.

The Five C's of Effective Communication

A great way to determine whether you're communicating effectively is by considering the five C's. These are speech qualities that help you to be an effective communicator. Applying these five C's to your communication style can help you talk to others in your life more effectively, which will help you to build relationships and appear confident. Understanding the five C's and how important they are for effective communication will help you to learn how to integrate them into your everyday speech.

Be Concise

The first C to consider is being concise. Have you ever talked to someone who goes on and on, and never seems to reach the point of their story? Although you don't want to be rude, it can be quite draining to listen to, and it also doesn't leave you much space to talk. This can make you leave the conversation with a negative impression of the other person, as they talked all the time and showed no interest in hearing from you.

When you want to communicate something, you need to avoid being too wordy. Going off track and taking too much time to say what you're thinking can end up losing the person you're talking to. Many people don't have the time or attention span for long-winded communication that leaves them no time to speak, so they want to hear the point of your story quickly, instead of hearing you ramble too long. Here are some tips that will help you to be a more concise communicator:

- **Avoid irrelevant tangents.** You may have something specific to talk about, but when you begin to talk, you start going off on a tangent and bringing up things that are irrelevant. It can be easy to get mentally distracted, and bring up other topics that relate to what you're talking about. However, you need to avoid going off on tangents that don't add to what you're speaking about. When you go off on too many tangents, you end up unsure what the objective of your story was in the first place.
- **Prevent over-explaining.** When you're telling a story or explaining a situation in your conversation, it can be difficult to be concise. You may find yourself explaining the finer details of the story that no one actually needs to know. You need to

give the person you're talking to some credit, as they will be able to fill in the blanks of your explanation. Over-explaining something only makes the conversation run longer, and it can also be less interesting to listen to. Keeping your explanations concise and clear helps people to remain engaged and interested in what you have to say.

- **Don't use filler words.** Another reason why you may find yourself talking for too long and being less concise is if you use filler words frequently. Examples of filler words include "like," "um," and "so." When you use filler words, it can influence you to think of more things to say, that may not be necessary for the conversation. It's a sign that you are thinking of more details or ideas to add to your story that may not need to be contributed. You should avoid using these filler words, as they make you less concise.

Be Clear

The next C is being clear, which can help you to be more concise. When you speak with clarity, you should make sure your words are concise and to the point. This will prevent you from rambling and adding unnecessary elements to the conversation. Speaking with clarity can also help others understand you more. You want to be able to communicate in a way that makes sense to all the people you talk to, so finding ways to be more clear when you speak can help your communication become a lot more effective. Here are some ways you can communicate with more clarity:

- **Take pauses.** Rambling, overexplaining, and confusing speech are all products of rushing when you speak. You may be feeling fearful or anxious in a situation, which impacts how you communicate with others. This causes you to talk fast without breaks, or use filler words, and you end up communicating ineffectively. It's important for you to take the necessary pauses, so you can think properly before you speak.

- **Be specific.** If you want to be more clear when you communicate, you need to be more specific with what you say. You want your communication to be specific so that it's easy to understand. You need to think about what you're talking about before you speak so that you can have more specific communication. Have specific points you want to convey before you go into the conversation, so you can stick to the specifics. You can also use examples to help you stay clear and concise as you communicate something.
- **Speak objectively.** When you find yourself in conflict with someone, speaking clearly is essential. You need to be able to put your emotional reactions aside, so you can explain your side of the story in a clear and objective manner. Being objective helps you to leave

your emotions out of the situation, so you can speak with logic and facts. When you clearly explain your side of the story, it makes it easier for the other person to understand your position, which can help you to resolve the conflict in a healthy manner.

- **Articulate yourself well.** If you want to be an all round clear communicator, you should consider how you can physically communicate with more clarity. How you speak to people impacts how well they receive it, as they might not hear what you're saying properly, which can lead to miscommunications and not understanding each other. To physically speak with more clarity, you must work on how you pronounce and enunciate your words. You also need to speak slowly in a good pitch, so they can hear and process everything you say clearly.

Be in Control

Communication can feel daunting when you don't feel in control of the conversation; however, with the five C's of communication, you can learn how to regain control of conversations. You are in control of how you communicate, and this authoritative and confident tone and persona can help you direct the conversation to where you want it to be. These are some tips that will help you to be in control of your communication:

- **Guide the conversation.** There are different techniques we've already discussed throughout the book that can help you to guide the conversation to where you want it to be. If you are talking to someone, and you want to cover a specific topic, then you can use funnel questions, leading questions, or topic transitions to get your conversation to where you want it. You have the power to influence the conversation.

- **Communicate honestly and openly.** You can use techniques to guide the conversation to your chosen topic strategically, or you could just choose to communicate honestly and openly. It shows a lot of confidence to tell someone exactly what you want to talk about. When you do this, you need to make sure you speak in a respectful and friendly tone, because you don't want to come off too bossy or intense.

Be Courteous

However you choose to communicate to the people around you, you need to be polite while doing it. You want to leave a good impression with people, so regardless of how confident, in control, or clear you are with your speech, you need to also be courteous. Being polite to the people you talk to is essential, as you need to speak to others how you want them to speak to you. When you want to learn how to be more courteous when you communicate, you should utilize the following tips:

- **Saying "please," "thank you," and "sorry."** A big part of being polite when communicating is being able to say "please," "thank you," and "sorry" when it's necessary. Although this may seem obvious, you may be guilty of using these words without realizing it. Simply telling someone "thank you" when they do something nice for you can make them feel appreciated. Saying sorry genuinely when you've done something wrong shows respect and your ability to take accountability, and saying please makes people warm up to you. As small and simple as these words are, using them when necessary can show people how courteous and caring you are.
- **Don't interrupt others.** Although you may want the topic to be changed or you want to show your confidence, you should never interrupt when someone is talking. You need to be able to hold onto

your thoughts, and communicate them when it's your turn to speak. Interrupting people when they speak doesn't only look impolite, but it also makes the other person feel as though you're not even listening to them. You may be talking to someone who talks a lot, and this makes you want to interrupt, but you should find a polite way to say that you want some time to talk.

Be Confident

When you're working toward communicating effectively, confidence is key. People will be interested in whatever you have to say when they can see that you're truly confident in it. You may find that when you communicate with confidence, all the other four C's fall into place, as you're able to be in control, be concise and clear, as well as be courteous. Speaking with confidence comes from within, so these are some tips that will help you to become a confident communicator:

- **Consider your body language.** Your body language plays a big role in how confident you seem speaking. If you find yourself slouching with your arms crossed, it's a sign that you're insecure and shy while speaking. To appear more confident, you need to stand with great posture, with your head high and your shoulders back. Hand gestures are also a great way to show more confidence as you speak.
- **Don't talk with doubt.** The biggest hack to having confidence when you speak is faking it until you make it. You need to convince yourself that you are confident in yourself, so it's crucial that you don't talk with doubt. Anytime you find yourself using a tone or phrase that shows doubt in your communication, remember to find your confidence again! One way to avoid sounding doubtful is by avoiding making statements as if they are questions.

When you use this inquiry-like tone to make a statement, it shows that you don't trust what you're saying.
- **Practice breathing exercises.** If you find yourself truly overwhelmed by speaking to others, then you should do some breathing exercises to calm yourself down. Being calm as you speak will help you communicate more confidently. Breathing in and out deeply can help you to calm down, so you can approach any conversation or communication obstacle with confidence. Using breathing exercises will also help you to articulate and pronounce your words better.

It's important to note that the five C's can be different in other sources, as they can mean different things to other people. However, these five C words are the most suitable for learning effective communication through this book. You need to learn how to take back **C**ontrol of your life, so you can be a **C**onfident communicator who speaks with **C**larity.

Being **C**oncise during communication helps others to understand, but above all, to be an effective communicator, you must be **C**ourteous and kind! Understanding these five C's will help you to evolve into the effective communicator you were meant to be.

Speech Problems and Fears

Do you find yourself struggling with specific speech obstacles that hold you back from communicating effectively? If so, you're not alone, as there are many people who struggle with these obstacles and blockages, as communication can be challenging and complex. It's important not to let your fears hold you back, so you can be the confident and effective communicator you were meant to be.

Communication Obstacles and How to Overcome Them

What communication obstacles have you come across in your life, and how did you overcome them? We all experience some obstacles when communicating, so it's important not to beat yourself up about it. Instead of letting these obstacles defeat you, you must first discover what they are. These are the four communication barriers that may be holding you back:

- **Physical barriers.** The biggest challenge to overcome are physical barriers. These physical barriers include hearing issues, as people may not be able to physically hear what you're trying to tell them. You could be talking to someone who has a mute disability, which makes them unable to verbally respond to you. When you come across people who can't physically understand you because of their impediments, you need to be more patient as you find alternative ways to communicate with them.
- **Language barriers.** If English is your second language, you may find that communicating some things you

know how to say in your mother tongue come out weirdly in English. This can make people misunderstand what you're trying to say to them. Or vice versa, as you may be trying to speak to someone who speaks English as their second language, and this makes it hard for you to understand what they're trying to say to you most of the time.
- **Cultural differences.** A major communication obstacle that many people face is having cultural barriers, as this can make it challenging for you to understand others. In different cultures, there are various phrases or sayings that are used. You may use your cultural ideas and phrases while communicating, which can confuse others who don't understand your culture.
- **Psychological barriers.** The last barrier you may be struggling with is a psychological one. This is when you're thrown off your communication mentally, as you can

see the other person shows no interest in what you're talking about. Your mind perceives whether someone is interested in a conversation or not, and the same is done when someone else is talking to you. This is why body language and responses are important, so that both parties can feel psychologically engaged in the conversation.

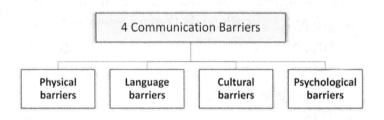

Once you identify what type of communication barrier you may be struggling with, you can find more practical ways to overcome them. Understanding what type of communication obstacles you have gives you an idea of how to solve these problems. No obstacle can be fixed without the right communication. These are a few ways you can look into solving communication obstacles:

- **Translating yourself.** Unfortunately, having a cultural and language barrier can make it challenging to get on the same page as others who don't speak the same language as you. This challenge can be overcome by trying your best to translate yourself. Use these communication tips to communicate what you're thinking in the best way possible. You can also inform the people you're talking to that you have cultural and language differences, so they should be patient with you.
- **Clearing up miscommunication.** As established earlier, miscommunications can be one of the biggest causes of conflicts and relationship obstacles. Unfortunately, life can be filled with miscommunications at times, which are challenging to prevent, but there is an easy way to clear them up before conflict breaks loose. You need to use effective communication

to calmly and reasonably explain miscommunications. This helps both parties make sense of the situation before arguments start.
- **Provide a disclosure.** You may have a different way of communicating that other people don't understand, which sets an obstacle in the way of your communication. There's nothing wrong with communicating differently than others, but if you want to avoid being misunderstood, you can use a disclosure. Let the other person know that you have a different way of communicating, but you say everything with good intentions. This disclosure will help to prevent any unnecessary conflict.

How to Kill a Conversation

Regardless of what your communication obstacles and blockages may be, you need to learn how to have a good conversation. You can't let this fear prevent you from having genuine and successful conversations that help you to build relationships, diffuse conflict, and get you further in life. Do you find yourself being a conversation-killer who makes the atmosphere awkward and uncomfortable? Being a conversation-killer can increase your fears and obstacles, making you an ineffective communicator. These are some ways you may find yourself killing a conversation, as well as tips that can prevent you from doing it:

- **Labeling people.** Making assumptions, judging, and labeling people is a quick way to kill a good conversation. People don't like to be grouped or generalized, as we are all our own individual beings. When you label someone in a conversation, it may end up offending them, especially if you do it negatively during conflict. Even if you're labeling someone else and not the person you're talking to, it's not a good presentation for you.

- **Constantly complaining.** It's normal to feel the need to complain to someone at times, but you can't spend the entire conversation complaining to someone. If you're upset about a situation, you can mention it and complain, but don't make the conversation all about you, and how unhappy you are. This can become extremely boring and frustrating for the other person, as they don't want to constantly hear about your complaints. Make sure you leave the floor open for two-way communication by asking them what their opinion is about the situation you're talking about.
- **One-upping the other person.** When you find yourself having a discussion with someone about their life accomplishments, you need to express how happy you are for them. If you are a very competitive or jealous type of person, you may find yourself trying to one-up the other person without even realizing it. When you one-up someone, you

constantly find something to say about yourself that makes you seem better than them. For example, if the other person tells you about a competition they won, you may bring up an even more prestigious competition that you won. You need to give other people their moment to shine, or else they won't want to communicate with you.

How to Manage Your Communication Fears

One of the best ways to accomplish more effective communication is by getting to the bottom of your fears. You may learn hundreds of tips and tricks that can help you be a more confident communicator, but you will never make true improvement if you don't manage and tackle your fears about communication. You need to be able to determine what your fears about communication are so that you can get rid of them for good. Following these steps will help you to conquer your communication fears:

1. **Determine what fears you have.** Do you have fears and anxieties when you are required to communicate? If you feel yourself having these negative feelings toward any form of conversation, it's a sign that you have fears that you need to conquer. It's important for you to discover what these fears could be, as there are many different reasons for the fear. For example, you may have a fear of embarrassing yourself around people; or, communicating makes you anxious because you crumble under pressure. You need to be able to determine where your fear is coming from, so you can have a specific obstacle to tackle.
2. **Consider why you have them.** Finding the reason behind why you have communication fears can help you to tackle them. Our fears all develop from somewhere, so if you take the time to think hard enough,

you can get to the root of the issue. You may find that you've developed a fear of talking to more than one person at a time because someone told you you're an awkward person who doesn't know how to socialize. Knowing where your fears originate from can help you to realize that your anxiety or stress about communication is unwarranted

3. **Throw yourself into the deep end.** The best way to overcome this fear is by throwing yourself into the deep end. You can find ways to mentally warm up to the idea of getting out of your comfort zone, but challenging yourself will get you the best results. Getting out of your comfort zone is all about diving into the deep end and doing things you're fearful of. If you're scared to ask someone out on a date, or start a friendship, then you should find the best way to approach exactly this communication obstacle.

4. **Realize it's not so scary.** Once you throw yourself into the deep end

you'll realize that your fears aren't as scary as you thought they were. You may feel embarrassed or scared, but the result of the situation won't be as bad as you thought it would've been. Coming to this realization can help you tackle all of your communication fears. You'll also start to realize that communication is all about being confident about yourself. If you trust yourself and pursue what you want through communication, you can't go wrong!

Practicing Self-Awareness

Having self-awareness plays a big role in how you communicate. When you're self-aware about how you talk to others, it can tell you a lot about yourself, as well as help you discover whether you have effective communication skills or not. Many people go through each day communicating automatically, without considering their words and how they affect other people.

The Importance of Self-Awareness

If you want to improve your communication skills and become more confident and effective with how you speak to others, you need to practice self-awareness. We all know the person who can be extremely rude and hurtful with their words, but they never apologize, and don't even realize when they're in the wrong. Although you may not be as extreme as this example, it is still important for you to be self-aware of how you communicate.

You may be unaware of some unhealthy conversation habits you have such as interrupting others, avoiding questions, or not thinking before speaking. Being aware of how you sound from an external point of view can help you to realize why you're having trouble communicating, as well as how it's impacting your current and developing relationships.

Being self-aware can also help you to recognize where and how you need help with your communication skills. This prevents you from saying things that you would probably end up regretting in the long run. Having self-awareness can also help you to reflect on how you communicated in the past, which helps you identify where you need to improve.

How to Be More Self-Aware

Finding self-awareness comes from within, as it requires you to monitor how you talk, behave, and respond to the people around you at all times. You're able to find patterns of behavior with your communication, and you're the only person who can understand why you communicate the way you do. Learning how to practice self-awareness will benefit you greatly on your journey toward achieving effective communication. Here are some tips that will help you to be more self-aware of your communication:

- **Being mindful.** We all think thousands of thoughts throughout the day, which influence the things we say. You need to be mindful of these thoughts, and how they translate into words, as they could be making a bigger impact on your life than you may realize. Practicing mindfulness helps you to identify when you say something that may be hurtful and offensive to the person who you're communicating with.
- **Pay attention to your emotions.** It can be challenging to identify when you are communicating negatively, so paying attention to your emotions can help you to be aware of how you're communicating. Whether you like to admit it or not, at some point in your life you've let your emotions control the way you communicate. When you notice yourself feeling more emotional, observe how you communicate in these moments. If you find yourself

reacting negatively because of your emotions, you should try to find healthy ways to communicate how you're feeling instead of lashing out.
- **Ask for feedback.** Sometimes we can be ignorant about our own behavior, as it's difficult to recognize when we're in the wrong. This makes it valuable for you to ask for feedback from others, so you can see things from a different perspective. Tell the other people in your life to be honest with you by expressing your communication flaws, and how they feel when they talk to you. Hearing about your communication from another person can also provide you with a reality check, as you're more inclined to believe someone else's experience with you.

Staying Attentive to Mannerisms

If you're working on practicing self-awareness, you should work on being more attentive to your mannerisms as well Your mannerisms play a big role in how effectively you communicate with others. If you want to be perceived in a positive light, you need to be able to use your body language to your advantage. These are some ways you can be attentive and aware of your mannerisms:

- **Being mindful of your posture.** As mentioned earlier, your posture plays a big role in how effectively you communicate with others. If you want to appear confident and positive, you need to ensure your posture exudes this energy. Throughout your different conversations during the day, you should seek awareness of your posture so you can prevent yourself from slouching and sitting or standing inappropriately in front of other people.
- **Consider your facial expressions.** The facial expressions you use as you communicate have an impact on how

well your communication is perceived. People evaluate your mannerisms as you communicate, as they can help them see in what type of tone you're talking. When you have a serious and concerned face, they may think what you're saying is important, but if you're smiling and look cheerful, they'll think what you're saying is more light-hearted. Ensure that your facial expressions align with the context of your communication, as it can add more accurate context to the conversation!

- **Notice the other person's mannerisms.** Did you know that we mirror each other when we speak quite often? If you want to be more attentive to your mannerisms, you should keep a look out on the other person's mannerisms. You may find what they're doing with their body language reflects what you're doing. So, if you can see the person that you're with is more closed off with their body language, look at how you're positioned. You want to have more open and friendly body language and facial expressions, so the person you're talking to can reciprocate the same energy.

CHAPTER 5

Indirectly Influencing Others

"You must be able to communicate successfully in order to become a leader and someone others listen to." – Keith Boyer

Have you ever met someone who has an influential and charismatic energy? How they communicate persuades you into believing their ideas and opinions. What if you were told that there are specific psychological tricks that can help you to influence others indirectly? You don't have to be a mind reader or hypnotist to influence how others think, as this can simply be achieved with the power of communication.

Psychological Tricks

Looking at the psychological side of communication can help you to find ways to communicate in a more influential manner. How we talk to others has a deeper impact on them than we may realize. When responding to you, they may be verbally communicating one thing, but their thoughts are thinking something else. This means that you can use your communication to win over other people psychologically, which in return will get you the verbal and physical results you desire.

Psychological Tricks for Effective Communication

Many people have communication tips and tricks that help them to get and hear what they want in life. You have the power to use your words to get what you desire in a situation. These are some psychological tricks you can use for effective communication, which will also help you to indirectly influence others:

- **Don't be too pushy for information.** If you want to get more information from the person you're talking to because you feel like they have a secret or something important they're keeping from you, don't be pushy by bombarding them with questions. When you become pushy and forceful, the other person will know what you're trying to do immediately, and they won't come out with the truth. The best truth serum is letting the other person continuously talk freely on their own. When you just let the other person talk ,and act as though you're not eager to hear, the truth may end up coming out accidentally.
- **Calming someone down.** If you're in a chaotic and stressful situation and the person you're talking to is freaking out, you'll find that it's impossible to talk to this person. If you want to de-escalate and calm this person down, using

this psychology trick will help. You should ask this person questions about their personal life or something that includes numbers. Doing this will distract their mind from the situation at hand, as they have to focus their mind on answering the question. After they answer a set of these questions, you'll find that they're a lot easier to talk to.

- **Saying you understand.** When you find yourself in conflict with someone and they begin to get angry, there's an easy way to diffuse this conflict. Sometimes all the other person needs to hear is that they're being understood in the moment. They may get annoyed and frustrated, which causes them to lash out, but all they want to hear in that moment is that you're listening, you understand, and you care. Simply telling them "I completely understand" can make them calm down and the conflict gets diffused. In life you have to pick your battles,

and know when it's time to leave an argument behind.
- **Avoid repeating yourself.** Do you find yourself having the same monotonous conversations with an individual in your life because they failed to listen to you the first time? This psychological hack will prevent anyone from forgetting what you asked or told them. When you tell someone something, and they either ask you to repeat yourself or they don't listen to what you have to say, you must stare at them in the eye for a few seconds while they look at you. You can then proceed to tell them again, and after that they will remember what you told them!

How To Practice Psychological Tricks

When you are learning how to influence others indirectly through communication, you need to be able to be direct enough to influence them, but you can't be too obvious that they know you're trying to persuade them. This makes it crucial for you to learn how to use dialogue tactically. These examples of dialogue will help you learn how to utilize the previous psychology tricks.

Example 1 - Calming Down Conflict

For this example, you can see how to use tactical dialogue to diffuse conflict and tension with someone.

Partner: *I'm so upset that you lied to me about where you were. How could you do this to me? Would you just like to break up since you don't respect me enough to tell me the truth?*

You: *I'm so sorry for not being honest with you. I completely understand why you were upset, and you have every right to feel the way you do. I love you so much, and it'll never happen again.*

Partner: **Thank you.**

This is the perfect way to calm down a tense situation. If you find someone else getting heated and saying hurtful things they don't really mean because they're upset with you, you must avoid getting offended and engaging in more conflict. Instead, you must show your understanding, and then it will be impossible for the other person to be mad with you and argue more. It's a quick and efficient way to diffuse most fights that seem to be escalating.

Example 2 - Neutralizing Stressful Work Situation

This example will help you calm down stressful situations by using psychological tricks to distract the stressed-out individual.

Colleague: *The boss is really upset with us. I'm so scared he's going to fire me because this is my second mistake this month. What am I going to do?!*

You: *How's your husband doing, and what does he do for work again?*

Colleague: *He's doing well I guess, and he's a chartered accountant. Is my career done in this office?!*

You: *What is your favorite restaurant to go to with your husband?*

Colleague: *It's this really romantic restaurant down the road. We go there for every anniversary.*

You: *That's beautiful. When you feel yourself getting freaked out by this work situation, try to imagine yourself on a romantic date with your husband at that restaurant.*

Colleague: *Thank you, it's actually helping!*

This example shows how you can use questions to distract people from getting too hysterical, and consumed by their own stress. You can help distract someone stressed by bringing up personal topics they care about. In this example, you used your colleagues' marriage and love as a positive distraction. This helps the other person to calm down, so you can have a more rational and calm conversation about everything.

Assertive Communication

As stated earlier, learning how to become an assertive communicator is important, as it helps you to become an effective communicator. You need to learn how to be more assertive when you communicate, so you speak with confidence and dominance in a conversation. People are more likely to be influenced by someone who is an assertive communicator, as they will believe in what you say.

Assertive Communication Skills

You may find that you're not a naturally assertive communicator, and that's okay.

Not everyone knows how to communicate with assertiveness, but this doesn't mean you can't learn. Finding ways to integrate assertive communication skills into your conversations can help you to become a more influential and persuasive individual. Over a time of using these assertive communication skills, you'll find yourself becoming more naturally assertive and confident. These are some assertive communication skills you should practice frequently.

- **Repeated assertion.** Being assertive means that you're not afraid to repeat yourself. You need to be able to reinforce your words to get your message across to others. This is where the communication skill of repeated assertion comes in handy. To emphasize the point you're making to someone to influence them, you must repeat yourself frequently. You should find calm ways to repeat yourself, and stick to the topic. When you do this, the other person will see how serious

you are about this topic, and they will begin to gain more interest.
- **Ask for time.** If you find yourself getting really emotional about something, you should ask for time before you try to communicate about the situation. Having time to calm down and understand the situation can help you to see both sides of the situation. This prevents you from talking irrationally in the moment, which can cause conflict and damage relationships. Asking for time to talk about a conversation gives you enough time to help you discover how you will approach the situation. You can then speak with logic and rationality, which will be respected by the other person. Just because you ask for time, doesn't mean you must forget about the situation and let it slide, as you need to be assertive and speak your mind!
- **Fogging.** Fogging is a technique that is used to diffuse conflict. It is done by either agreeing with truth to avoid responding in a way that

results in more conflict, or you give the other person space before the situation escalates anymore. To be a respected assertive communicator, you also need to have moments where you admit your wrong doing. Many people who communicate assertively have too much pride to admit when they're wrong. You may also find yourself in a conversation where you feel attacked by someone else's words, but you can't let your confidence and ego cause you to lash right back. This makes it valuable to use the fogging technique, to prevent any conflict from occurring. You should be able to take on criticism positively, even if it's delivered with aggression. This approach shows other people that you are able to admit when you're wrong, which can make them respect you even more.

- **Behavior rehearsal.** You may find yourself trying to apply all of these skills and previous tips given to be more assertive when communicating, but when you find yourself in a conversation, you crumble under pressure. No matter how hard you try, you aren't assertive like you planned in your head. This makes it valuable for you to rehearse your assertive communication skills and techniques before taking them out into the real world. You can practice being assertive by yourself, or you can ask a good friend or family member to help you. The more you practice being assertive, the more comfortable you will be at practicing it with everyone you meet.

How Using Assertive Communication Skills Helps

You may be wondering how exactly using these assertive communication skills will get you what you want from others: being assertive can help you to present the best version of yourself. If you want to influence others, you need to show them that you are a believable and confident individual. You will find that being assertive can help you to communicate persuasively in the following ways, which will allow you to influence those around you through conversations:

- If you want to influence people, you need to be able to gain their respect. People are more likely to listen to and believe individuals they trust. When you use assertive communication skills, you command a room verbally, and people respect what you're saying. This respect makes them more easily convinced by what you say, as well as more likely to agree with your ideas or opinions.
- Believe it or not, people can discover how you feel about yourself through the way you communicate with others. If you want to appear confident, with high self-esteem, then using assertive communication skills is perfect. The people you talk to will

think to themselves that you know what you're talking about because of how confident and sure of yourself you are. This makes you more convincing and influential, as people only want to follow individuals who believe in themselves.
- You are more influential when people understand what you're trying to say easily. You need to articulate yourself in a way that is concise and clear, so the person you're talking to understands exactly what you're trying to say. When you utilize your assertive communication skills, you will notice that you get straight to the point. This helps the other person understand what you're trying to say, and you end up being on the same page. Being assertive helps you to be concise, which many people appreciate during conversations.

How to Use Assertive Communication in

Dialogue

Although you may have a better idea of how you should carry yourself or behave to communicate assertively, you may still not know how to use assertiveness in dialogue. This is especially difficult if you're new to being assertive, and you don't know how to do it with confidence without sounding rude or arrogant. These dialogue examples will help you to integrate assertive communication into your everyday conversations:

Example 1 - Being Assertive During Conflict

In this example, you can see how you can use assertive communication to stand your ground in a respectful manner during moments of conflict.

Friend: It doesn't even matter that I told other people about your secret. Why do you care?

You: It's important to me, as that secret was very personal to me. I don't appreciate how you broke this boundary in our friendship.

Friend: *But no one cares about your stupid secret.*

You: *That isn't the point, as I told you about it in confidence. I would really appreciate it if you kept my secrets to yourself from now on.*

Friend: *I won't tell anyone else, I'm sorry. It was wrong of me to tell other people about something private you trusted me with.*

In this example, you can see how valuable it is to stand up for yourself respectfully. You don't need to scream and shout, or say something hurtful to win an argument. All you need to do is express calmly how you feel. Even if the other person doesn't understand, and continues to say hurtful things, you need to continue to emphasize your point of view with confidence.

Example 2 - Communicating With Confidence

Being an assertive communicator is all about communicating with confidence, so this is an example of how you can show confidence through your conversations.

New Friend: *I really hate Rebecca. She's so annoying and I can't believe how she dresses. Disgusting.*

You: *I'm actually friends with Rebecca, and she's a lovely person.*

New Friend: *You're friends with her? If you're close to her you can't be a part of our group anymore, so pick a side.*

You: *I'm going to stick with Rebecca. I don't want to be friends with people who bring others down.*

In this example, you are building friendships with a new group of people, which is important for you because you're trying to fit in. However, when you see them insulting someone else you care about, you use your assertive communication to stand up for them. This shows confident and assertive communication, as you stand up for what's right, while still being respectful and honest.

Irrefusable Offers

You may be trying to get an idea or opinion across to someone. You want to use your assertive behavior to convince other people to agree with what you're communicating. The best way to communicate with someone to get them to agree with you is by giving them an irrefusable offer. You need to offer them something important, in a way that it can't be refused.

What Do You Have To Offer?

What idea, opinion, or decision are you trying to convince others to accept?

Knowing what your offer is can help you to communicate it in a way that it can't be refused. You should understand the purpose and reasons behind an offer, so you can determine exactly how to make it irrefusable. These are some questions you should ask yourself about your offer:

- **What offer do you want to convince someone about?** Consider the offer you have in mind. You may want to ask for permission to do something, or you want to convince someone to agree with your decisions. Before you even ask for permission, acceptance, or agreement, you need to get your story straight by considering what it is you're actually asking for.
- **Why do you want to convince this person?** Once you come up with an offer, you need to determine why you want to convince this person. There must be a reason that motivates you to find approval and acceptance from someone else. Maybe you can't go through with a decision without getting approval

from a certain individual, so you need to convince this person to get what you want.
- **How important is this offer?** You should then ask yourself how important this offer actually is. Knowing the intensity of the matter can help you to determine how irrefusable you need to make your offer. You can determine how much you need to push this offer on someone, by considering the importance of the outcome.

How to Make an Offer Irrefusable

Once you've discovered what your offer is and why you're proposing it, you can then determine how you'll make it irrefusable. Knowing how to make an offer impossible to refuse can help you to influence others to agree with you in life. This is a valuable skill to have in life, as you can get what you want with the use of the right words. These are some steps that can help you make an offer irrefusable:

1. **Sell your offer.** If you want to ensure that the person you're talking to loves your offer, you need to be able to sell it. You can't just casually bring it up, and expect them to agree with you. To sell your offer, you need to put some effort into how you communicate about it. You should emphasize how important it is by repeating your offer, as well as think of some benefits of your offer that will convince them to get onboard with the idea.
2. **Explain its importance.** If your offer is truly important, and needs to be agreed upon, you need to go the extra mile by convincing the other person how important it truly is. You need to make them aware that their agreement plays a massive role, and how this offer can be advantageous to them. For example, if the offer is to take a business trip, but your partner doesn't want you to go, you need to explain how important it is.

Maybe the business trip is essential for employees to get the opportunity to get a promotion. If you get a promotion, it'll be beneficial for you and your partner. Translating things into their terms will help them understand how irrefusable the offer truly is.

3. **Avoiding demanding.** Although you may really want something from this offer, you need to avoid being forceful. This may be an important situation, but being forceful and demanding isn't the way to get things in life. When you command people around you, you make it seem like you're demanding they follow your lead. People don't appreciate being bossed around, so you need to make sure you're making your offer irrefusable in an indirect manner.

CHAPTER 6

Making Your Words Effective

"The quality of your communication determines the size of your result." – Meir Ezra

If you truly want to make an impact with your words, you need to be able to recognize the power behind them. If you want to use communication to influence others, build relationships, and diffuse conflict, you need to put emotion and feelings behind your words. It's also important to let your actions speak for you, to prove how genuine you are with your words.

Connect Emotions to Your Message

Words can feel really empty and meaningless when emotions aren't connected to it. People want to see that you truly care about what you're talking about, as this convinces them about what you're saying. If you're trying to state your case in an argument, or give someone a better understanding of you, or merely have a casual conversation, you need to have emotions beyond your words.

The Power of Speaking With Emotions

Have you ever had a conversation with someone who has a monotonous and dreary voice? It can feel as though they are talking for hours, and you struggle to actually focus on what they're trying to say. Not only are they difficult to focus on, but they also seem like they don't care about what they're talking about.

Although they may be super passionate about what they're talking about, you'll never know it because of the lack of emotion in their tone.

Using emotions in your message is highly valuable, as it helps the other person to put your words in more context and understand them. It makes a bigger impact and impression on other people when you talk with emotions and passion. These are some benefits of communicating with emotions:

- **Influencing others.** It's a lot easier to influence people when they can see how passionate you are about something. No one will believe in what you have to say when you seem like you don't care about yourself. When you put the right emotions into your words, you will give people the right message in a way that sounds more convincing. By doing this, you'll find that you successfully influence others.
- **Becoming more relatable.** When people see you talking with

genuine emotions, you become more human to them. Seeing someone react to life emotionally in a similar way would make you feel more normal for being emotional in the first place. It's difficult for people to understand you and how you feel about something when you don't express emotions, so when they see you using emotions when you talk, they're able to understand and relate to what you're saying and going through.

- **Bonding over the negatives.** If you're building a relationship with someone, you want to show you can be human, and vulnerable with your emotions, whether they're good or bad. Being able to be vulnerable by showing your negative emotions and circumstances in your life can help you to bond a lot more. It gives the other person insight into who you are as a person, and they are able to get closer to you by comforting you through it all. Showing your emotions in your words also makes other people feel comfortable to open up to you when they're experiencing something negative.

As humans, it's easier for us to trust and believe others when they speak with suitable emotions. We empathize with those that experience emotional reactions similar to us in specific situations. Although it's crucial to speak with emotions, you don't want to exaggerate and overdo it. You want to have suitable emotional responses as you speak, that other people can empathize with.

How to Speak With Emotions

You may be the type of person who speaks with less expression and tone. Although this may be the natural way you speak, you need to find ways to add emotion to your words. If you want to be influential, charismatic, confident, and believable, you have to have the right emotions when you communicate. There are also different emotions you should be expressing for different situations. Learning how to speak with the right emotions at the appropriate moments can help you to have more effective communication. These are some ways you can speak with emotion:

- **Tone is everything.** The tone and expressions you use when you communicate have a major impact on how your communication is perceived. We all have different tones when we speak about various things, whether it's serious and monotonous, or bubbly and exciting. The most organic way to express your emotions through your words is by utilizing the right tone as you speak. Your tone can say a lot about how you feel toward what you're communicating.
- **Channel your emotions.** We all have emotions that are triggered by different experiences. You may get happy and excited every time you see a dog as you're a huge animal lover. On the other hand, someone

else might find happiness in seeing other people succeed. It's important to understand your emotions and where they come from, so you can channel them efficiently. When you're having a conversation with someone, consider to yourself what emotions you're feeling during the conversation. If you're talking about something that makes you excited, channel that energy, but if you're talking about something that causes you to become angry, find a healthy way to channel and express these negative emotions.

- **Expressing the right emotions.** Sometimes people say things in a conversation to get an emotional reaction from you. If they open up to you and get vulnerable, they probably want an emotional response that shows you care about them and what they're saying. This makes it important for you to express the right emotions at the right time. If you are having a conversation about something sad, you should express how upset you are through your emotions. You need to make sure that you are expressing an appropriate emotion at the right time in the conversation.

- **Avoid reacting.** Although it's important to put your emotions in your communication, you need to avoid using your emotions to react negatively. It's about finding a healthy balance that doesn't instigate unnecessary conflict. When you use your emotions to react negatively, you can say things you may regret later. For example, you may be feeling offended by what someone has said to you, which makes you respond in anger. You use your words with intense emotion to retaliate. Although it's what you wanted to do at the moment, after doing it you will end up regretting your emotionally hurtful reaction.

Showing emotions through your words is more than your facial expressions, body language, and tone, as it's the holistic way you carry yourself as you communicate. Even though you may think you don't speak with emotions, we all use emotions as we speak all the time. Getting in touch with the emotional side of yourself will help you to express your emotions in a more organic manner.

Actions Speak Louder Than Words

Words don't mean anything when you don't do the actions to back them. If you're the type of person who says one thing but does another, people will begin to lose faith in you. You need to prove your honesty, integrity, and good nature by using your actions to reflect your words. It's important to ensure that your words and actions work hand in hand.

The Value of Actions

Although words are lovely to hear, they are never as important as physical actions. You may love to hear compliments, reassurance, and promises from the people around you, but seeing these promises and words come to life through actions is even better! When talking about effective communication, we often forget how truly valuable actions are. These are some ways actions are valuable, as they validate and enhance the power of your words:

- **Shows honesty.** Being able to stick to your word shows honesty and integrity. When you're able to say something and display it through action, it's a testament that your words were true in the first place. Showing your honesty through actions consistently helps people realize that you're a person they can trust in their lives. It's difficult to just trust words, but when you see real life actions, it convinces you to trust this individual more.
- **Shows you care.** Putting actions into your words shows how much effort you're willing to put into a situation. Taking action by doing

something nice and generous for another person makes them feel special and cared for. Anyone can say something nice, but it takes a person who cares to actually act upon those words. You want to make people feel as though they are worth the effort of your actions!
- **Gets things done.** Not only does using actions instead of just words show that you're an honest and good person, but it also helps you to get things accomplished in your life. If you're constantly talking about doing this and doing that, these things will never actually be accomplished. You need to be an individual of action if you want to build relationships, excel in your career, and be the best version of yourself. Things only occur in life when you take action, instead of merely talking about things happening.

How to Be True to Your Word

Words are so easy to say. You can tell someone you'll do something for them, you can say you're going to change and be a better person, or you can use your words to express how you feel toward someone. However, these words don't mean anything if you don't do the actions required to fulfill them. If you're the type of person who is quick to say the right words, but never acts on them, it's time for this to change. Effective communication is about being honest about what you're saying, and this requires you to follow through with actions. These are some ways you can be more true to your word:

- **Consider your communication patterns.** To determine whether you follow through with your words or not, you need to consider your communication patterns. You need to take a look at how you communicate, and consider what you promise others, and what happens after that. Do you say things and shortly after prove it with action, or do you delay acting upon all of your promises? If

you notice that you've not been true to your word a couple times, that's normal, but if it's become an unhealthy communication pattern, it's important to conquer this issue.
- **Be honest with yourself and others.** You may think that you aren't guilty of making empty promises, saying things you don't mean, or telling lies, but it's crucial for you to be honest with yourself before you're able to be honest with others. You need to look at your communication patterns honestly, and consider whether you've let anyone down with your actions. Although you may want to say the right words that make others happy, you need to be honest, even if it's not what the other person wants to hear. People will appreciate the fact that you are being honest.
- **Force yourself to act.** On the other hand, you may be someone who struggles to commit to their words. You want to believe that you can follow through with your words,

but when it comes to acting on them, you struggle. Sometimes you just need to get yourself to act according to your words, so you don't disappoint yourself, or the people around you. When you promise you'll do something for someone, ensure that you set aside time to actually do it. If you tell someone you won't let them down, try your absolute best never to let them down. When you plan to do the things you talk about, it'll become habitual for you to turn your words into actions.

- **Don't say anything you don't mean.** It can be tempting just to tell someone what they want to hear at the moment. You want to make the other person happy, resolve conflict, or get what you want at that moment. But you must never say something you don't truly mean. If you feel like you want to make a promise, or say something that you don't entirely mean, stop yourself and be honest. When you convince people with your words and don't follow through with action, you will only end up upsetting them, and make yourself look dishonest.

At the end of the day, you're the only person who can deliver on their words. If you know you can't achieve or do something, you must avoid making empty promises. You want to build rapport and trust in your relationships, so you can build and grow emotional connections. The more you fail to deliver on your word, the less likely you are to get trusted by others.

CHAPTER 7

Practice Makes Perfect

"Communication works for those who work at it." – John Powell

Unfortunately, you're not going to learn how to be the perfect communicator overnight, so it's important to put in the work, and practice consistently. The more you work on your effective communication skills, the easier you will find communicating with others. It's important to keep on practicing effective communication, even if you feel like you're not making the progress you wanted.

Throughout this book, you've learnt various skills and techniques that you should use to accomplish effective communication. Although it's valuable to think about these skills and techniques, to become the effective, assertive, and confident communicator you want to be, you need to learn how to put the things you've learned into practice. This chapter will help you learn how to apply these skills to your everyday communication!

How to Put Your Skills Into Action

You need to be able to put all the above tips into action, so you can be a more effective communicator. The more you practice these tips and skills, the easier it will be for you to become an effective communicator. As you begin to practice these communication skills, you will find that you may struggle to get the hang of it at first, as you struggle to maintain your confidence. But with time, these skills will become second nature for you.

Practice Dialogues

If you are preparing yourself to have a conversation with someone you may feel nervous about, you may find it valuable to practice dialogues. Being intimidated by a conversation you know you're going to have can make you a nervous wreck once it comes time to communicate. The key to a successful conversation is being confident in yourself, and remaining calm throughout the conversation. This is what makes practicing dialogues ahead of time so valuable. The following dialogue examples can inspire you to create your own, so you can feel comfortable when the real conversation occurs.

Example 1 - Making a New Friend

For many people, the thought of making new friends can be extremely daunting, because having to start a conversation with a stranger can be stressful. You don't know how to make a good impression with this stranger, and talk about something they're interested in, so you feel intimidated everytime you know you need to make a new friendship. This dialogue can help you to conquer this fear, as you learn how to break the ice with a new friend. You've got a new job, and you're anxious about making new work friends. You go to the staff kitchen during your break, and see someone making a cup of coffee.

You: I'm also going to make some coffee! It's actually my third cup today ,and it's not even noon yet. Are you a coffee addict like me?

New colleague: Haha, yes I am! I'm trying to cut down how much coffee I drink, but I can be extremely intolerable without my daily dosage of caffeine.

You: I feel exactly the same way, haha! I'm (your name), it's my first day on the job. Do you have any tips for me to survive here?

New colleague: Well I'm not doing too well myself here. Why do you think I drink so much coffee?

You: I'm sorry to hear that. Is there any reason why you're struggling?

New colleague: *I'm just feeling really drained by my workload, and I don't know how long I can stomach it.*

You: *That really sucks. You need to look after yourself, and get some rest. You know what? I'll treat you to a spa day this weekend.*

New colleague: *Oh my gosh that sounds lovely! Thank you so much.*

You: *It's absolutely my pleasure; I'll text you the details. Also, feel free to come to me whenever you need to vent.*

There are many great communication skills that were utilized in this practice dialogue. Firstly, you started off with a good impression by being friendly and casual, making it easier for the other person to warm up to you. From there, you used the power of questions to break the ice and tension between you. This not only helped to build a connection, but you also showed them how compassionate you can be. This helps you to score an outside-of-work visit that can build your friendship even further. You also made sure that the other person was comfortable to talk openly about their problems.

Example 2 - Resolving Conflict

Being in a situation when both you and the other party in the conversation are wrong can be both good and bad. It's bad because it can lead to an uncontrollable argument from both sides, where no one is understanding the other person's point of view. However, it is good because it can end easily with healthy and effective communication. Instead of blaming each other for what you both did, rather have a healthy and mature conversation about it. This practice dialogue shows how you can produce an apology and remorse.

Friend: How could you do this to me? You promised that you would support me and my relationship. Why would you gossip about us to all of our friends, and tell them that it's not a real relationship?

You: I'm really sorry for what I did. I did tell our friends that your relationship doesn't seem real to me, and I was so wrong for saying that. I support you and whatever makes you happy in your life. I shouldn't have said what I did. Can you forgive me?

Friend: Thank you for taking accountability. I forgive you, but please never talk behind my back again.

You: I promise I will never do it again. I do have something to bring up with you as well. I heard that you were also gossiping about me to our friends saying that I'm just jealous and lonely, as well as that I'll never find love because of how bitter I am. Although I understand what I said was wrong, I really didn't appreciate you saying that to me in return.

Friend: You're right, that was a low blow because I was feeling upset. I shouldn't have said that either. Let's agree that we'll never gossip about each other again!

You: *Yes, I forgive you, and I agree. I really don't want to fight with you because you're my best friend.*

This conversation was a great way to settle conflict from two sides. Although you were both upset and hurt, you managed to both get the apologies you desired. By immediately apologizing for your wrongdoing, you settled the conflict immediately. Your friend couldn't get more aggravated after you took full accountability. It also helped to calm your friend down, so you could also get an apology for your side of the story. It is important to remember that even if you apologize first to someone, they may not be as remorseful to you. But you should be happy that you took accountability where it was due.

Example 3 - Giving a Pitch

You have a big presentation or pitch that you need to prepare for, but you're anxious that you're not going to do a good job. It can be daunting to present something in front of people, as you feel put on the spot. However, the great thing about giving a pitch or presentation is that you can plan what you're going to say, and you can rehearse it to your heart's desire. But one thing you can't rehearse by heart is how your superiors, colleagues, or moderators respond to your pitch. They could ask a variety of questions that may overwhelm you. This example shows you how you can handle questions in a tense situation.

Moderator: *Thank you for that lovely pitch. I just have a few questions for you. How does this new packaging style impact the environment?*

You: *Great question! Unfortunately, this packaging is made of standard plastic like the last one, so it doesn't have any environmental benefits. However, if we splurge a little more on the packaging budget, we can use biodegradable plastic that has the same effect, but it's perfect for the environment.*

Moderator: *I like that idea. Maybe we can look into that in greater detail. My* next question is, are there any budget cuts we can make to produce this packaging?

You: I haven't considered the specifics of the costs, so I'm not sure where we could cut some costs. But when I did my own calculations, I saw the cost comes within the budget you provided me with.

Moderator: Okay, great. My last question will be, is packing economically efficient?

You: My apologies, but could you explain what that means?

Unfortunately, you can't really predict exactly what the other person is going to ask you, but you can consider some things that would be valuable information for them. Having a rough estimate of what questions you'll be asked can make you feel more prepared when you go into the pitch. After asking yourself these test questions, you can do some more brainstorming, so that you can give accurate, well-thought answers.

In this example, you can see how you can answer questions you don't know the answer to. You found the best way to answer the questions, even though you didn't have a direct answer. For the last question, you were completely confused about what the moderator was trying to ask, but instead of trying to give a confusing answer, you asked politely for clarity. Never be afraid to ask for explanations or context, as it shows you are trying to answer the questions properly!

How to Recover a Conversation

When you're beginning to use the tips and tools throughout the conversation, you may make mistakes every now and then, and slip back into your ineffective communication habits. As a beginner, your biggest fear may be saying something wrong and messing up a conversation, but it's so important to realize that no conversation is irrecoverable. Whatever mistake you may find yourself making in a conversation, you can recover it with effective communication. These following steps can help you to recover a conversation when it begins to go south:

1. **Assess the damage.** You should first consider how bad the damage to the conversation truly is. Although you may feel mortified by what you've said, you may have not done or said anything that bad. You need to see how much work you need to put into redeeming the conversation, so considering the extent of the damage is crucial. For example, you may find that you constantly interrupted the other person as they spoke, and you can notice that they're getting visibly annoyed. Although this isn't good for a conversation, it can be recovered with the right actions and words.
2. **Apologize if necessary.** If you did something in a conversation that you should apologize for, then it's important for you to do so. You may

have said something offensive that hurt the other person, so apologizing can help salvage their impression of you. You need to have a sincere and authentic apology that shows how apologetic you truly are. In this scenario that was stated before, you can apologize to the person you're speaking to for interrupting them during conversation.

3. **Reset your conversation.** Resetting your conversation doesn't literally mean you must start from scratch, but rather that you mentally restart your train of thought. Get back into the mindset of being an effective communicator, so you can continue this conversation as a better speaker. When you do this, you should also focus on redeeming your mistake, by compensating it with effective communication skills. For this example mentioned previously, you can go out of your way to hear what the other person has to say, by asking them questions and listening attentively. This will

show them that you didn't mean to interrupt them and make them feel unheard.

Once you follow these steps after you slip up, you will be able to get back on track to an effective and successful conversation. Don't let this mistake knock your confidence, as this can make you give up on your conversation altogether. Remember that you won't become a perfect communicator overnight, so you're bound to make mistakes. As long as you try to redeem your mistakes with the previous steps, you won't have any trouble making good, effective conversations.

CHAPTER 8

Managing Conflict

"You never really understand a person until you consider things from his point of view." – Harper Lee

We've discussed some ways you can use effective communication to manage conflict in your life, but what are some more practical communication techniques you can use to diffuse conflict, as well as avoid it in your life? Learning how to effectively manage conflict with the right type of communication will help to benefit the relationships in your life. You will find yourself having less arguments, and you will experience more mature and healthy conversations.

Effective Conflict Resolution Techniques

Unfortunately, it can be so easy to find yourself in conflict with someone. You or someone else could misunderstand something that was said, and this results in unnecessary arguments. You may even say something in the heat of the moment that you didn't really mean, but it hurts the other person nonetheless. Conflict even occurs when people are frustrated by personal things happening in their lives. Although conflict is normal at times, you shouldn't engage in it, as it can spiral into bigger issues. The following effective conflict resolution techniques will help you to put an end to any conflict you're experiencing.

Accepting Healthy Disagreements

You may find yourself getting really upset about a situation because someone strongly disagrees with something you've said. But, it's important to realize that healthy disagreements aren't bad. We don't all have the same opinions and thoughts in life, and that's okay. You need to be able to respect others for their opinions in life, and maybe even try to hear things from their perspective.

Although you may see things or certain situations in one specific way, this doesn't mean that this is the whole truth. Other people have other perceptions that may clash with yours, but being able to accept and welcome disagreements helps you to have a healthier relationship with people. You're able to respect each other and your thoughts, even if you don't see eye-to-eye on certain topics or situations.

Don't Ignore Conflict

When conflict occurs between you and someone in your life, you may find yourself trying to avoid the situation because it makes you uncomfortable. You don't want to fight with this person because they are special to you, so you think the best way to preserve your relationship is by avoiding the conflict altogether. Actually, doing this is not only detrimental to your relationship, but it is really unhelpful for your communication skills.

Ignoring conflict doesn't make it magically disappear. Instead, the conflict and tension in your relationship becomes a looming threat that causes many other issues. When you suppress conflict, you will find that it creates tension and awkwardness between you and the other party. This can cause you to clash even more, as well as cause a drift in your relationship.

Not only does it make things tense between you, but you will also find that the other person's behavior doesn't improve. You will both make the same mistakes, disrespect each other's boundaries, and do or say the same hurtful things. Without healthy and open communication during conflict, you will never know what went wrong, and how to improve things in your relationships.

It's important to just face the conflict head on, without beating around the bush. Sit the other person down and open up to each other. You need to confront the conflict, and what happened, in order to resolve it and move forward in a more positive light!

Finding Resolutions Together

The best way to resolve conflict is by communicating together. You can't resolve arguments or fights by yourself, so you need to engage in healthy communication together. It may be challenging to resolve conflict together when there is still heated tension between you and the other individual, so this makes it valuable to spend some time apart before you work on resolving the situation together.

Once you've both had time to cool down and think, you can work on conflict resolution techniques together. Being able to communicate about what went wrong and how it happened can help you to understand each other's perspectives. This will result in both parties apologizing and taking accountability, which allows you to move forward in your relationship.

How to Reduce Conflict

Although conflict is normal in life, you want to find ways to reduce it. Finding yourself in a disagreement every now and then is not the end of the world, but if you notice yourself continuously butting heads with the people in your life, it may be a sign that you need to work toward reducing conflict. You don't want to engage in continuous conflict, as this can be damaging for your relationships. The more you argue and disagree with the people in your life, the further you push them away from you.

Define Boundaries and Acceptable Behavior

People fight and get into arguments when they feel hurt, disrespected, or if their boundaries get broken. The best way to prevent this from happening is by having the important conversations about your boundaries and expected behavior from each other. You want to set a healthy standard that helps you to respect each other and your boundaries. These are some ways you can use effective communication to set healthy boundaries and acceptable behavior:

- **Communicate your boundaries openly.** You want to get the message across to the people in your life clearly that you want your boundaries to be respected. You can't expect people to read your mind and body language when you're uncomfortable with something, as some people aren't aware of social cues. You need to be able to openly and respectfully communicate what you dislike, and what makes you uncomfortable. You may be fearful to set boundaries in your close relationships in your life, but you may be surprised to find that it improves your relationships, as you treat each other with more respect and love.

- **Respect others' boundaries.** If you want the people in your life to respect your boundaries, you need to be able to respect their boundaries in return. You can't ask someone to respect your boundaries, and then refuse to respect their boundaries in return. When you have a conversation with someone about the boundaries and behavior you want in your relationship, you should provide them with the opportunity to express their boundaries. Learning about boundaries and behavior other people want from you can help you understand them, and what they're comfortable with.

- **Say "no" when you need to.** To reinforce your boundaries, you need to be able to say "no," and communicate when you feel a line is being crossed. You may be fearful of saying "no" to the people in your life because you don't want to disappoint anybody, but it's important to reinforce your boundaries. It can be easy for others to get into a habit of how they treat you, so they may slip back into old routines. This is when it's important to reinforce your boundaries by saying "no," and bringing it to their attention. The more you put a stop to your boundaries being broken, the less it'll happen, as the people in your life will adapt to it.

You'll find that setting your boundaries and acceptable behavior in a respectable way annihilates many issues that instigate arguments. You learn how to love and respect each other more, which helps you to have a healthier relationship with less conflict.

Provide Constructive Criticism

When you find yourself disagreeing with someone, or you want to get your point across to them, utilizing constructive criticism is the most effective way to go. Just because you want to avoid conflict doesn't mean you should avoid voicing your opinion altogether. You need to be able to tell people when they're wrong, and provide your advice. Using constructive criticism is the best way to accomplish this, as you make people aware of how you feel in a healthy and helpful way.

The best way to provide constructive criticism is by wording it with the other person's emotions in mind. Instead of just blurting out your criticism, you must consider how to say it in a way that doesn't hurt their feelings. You should try to focus on talking about the situation, instead of making it seem like you're criticizing the individual. This will make it feel less personal, and more helpful to the other person.

For example, if you don't like the actions or behavior of someone, when you provide constructive criticism about it you must focus your opinion on their physical actions, rather than bringing up their personality and motives.

You should also consider timing when you provide constructive criticism, as you want to ensure that you're bringing it up at a suitable time. Firstly, you need to provide constructive criticism at the time of the event, otherwise it will seem irrelevant when you bring it up at a later stage. However, although it's important to provide constructive criticism promptly, you should also ensure the atmosphere and vibe of the moment is right for criticism. If you can sense that the atmosphere is too tense, you should wait for the dust to settle and the situation to calm down, before providing your healthy criticism.

What makes criticism more constructive is when you provide ways in which the other person can improve. If you're going to tell someone their opinion is wrong, they did something in the wrong way, or their behavior is unhealthy, you need to provide them with ways they can correct it. If you just tell someone what's wrong about their actions and words, they will feel attacked, but if you give them constructive advice, they will understand your perspective. This can also help them to correct their behavior or words in the future.

Learning How to Express Anger

Another way you can work toward reducing conflict is by learning how to communicate your anger in a healthy manner. Being angry and frustrated at times can cause you to say or do things you don't really mean. You react to the intense emotions you're feeling, and end up taking it out on someone who doesn't deserve it. Whatever reason you have for being angry, you need to work toward managing it, and expressing it in a healthy way that doesn't hurt the people around you. This is a guide that will help you to identify your anger, so you can know how to communicate it in a healthier manner:

1. **Identify your anger.** The first step is being able to determine when you're getting angry, and consider how it's making you feel. The best way to identify your anger is by monitoring your behavior, as this can usually show how intense your anger truly is, and how well you're dealing with it. For example, you may find yourself yelling and screaming at someone who made you angry. Or, you could be identifying the earlier stages of your anger when you're clenching your fists and breathing heavily. It is better to identify your anger sooner than later, as it is easier to manage and express.
2. **Calm yourself down.** Once you identify yourself getting really angry,

you should find some ways to calm yourself down, so you don't end up reacting in a way you might regret. You need to be able to calm yourself down in order to express yourself in a healthier manner. You can accomplish this by practicing some breathing exercises, and visualizing something that brings you peace and happiness. By doing this, you're able to calm yourself, which prevents you from lashing out with anger.

3. **Move away from the situation.** You may find that your emotions and anger feel really intense in that moment, and simply doing breathing exercises doesn't cut it. If you are feeling overwhelmed by your anger at any point, you should move away from the situation, and get some space. Tell the person you're with that you need some time to yourself to cool off. Maybe go outside, go for a walk, or use your favorite music as a source of escapism. Moving yourself from the frustrating situation can help you to calm down and think

clearly, so you can come back and have a more civil and healthy conversation about everything.
4. **Express your emotions.** Once you've calmed yourself with the most suitable technique for you, then you can work on expressing your emotions to the other person. It's not healthy just to let the situation go altogether, as you were angry for a reason. This makes it valuable to have a calm conversation about how you felt in that, moment and why it triggered you. When you calmly express the frustration you feel, you're more likely to get your point across to the other person.

Once you follow these steps, you will be able to manage your anger and calm down, so you can channel your emotions in a healthier manner. It's all about being able to express how you feel to others with respect and honesty. You need to avoid blowing up and causing unnecessary conflict, which creates more problems.

Examples of Dialogue

Using effective communication when you find yourself within conflict can help you to eliminate the issue. Most of the time, conflicts get out of hand when both parties feel like they're not being heard or understood. This is why it's crucial to have conversations where you let each other speak your points of view. When doing this, you need to be able to actively listen to what the other person is telling you.

Hearing the other person's perspective, and taking accountability for what went wrong, will calm both of you down. You can then open up about your perspective, and you will find the other person becomes a lot less defensive. From there, you will find yourselves communicating more healthily, and resolving the tension between you. If you're not sure how this process can occur in a real-life conversation, then these following examples of dialogue will help you.

Example 1 - Using Constructive Criticism

If you find yourself in a position where you disagree with someone you're close with, or you have negative opinions on something they did, you may find that you don't want to tell them the truth. You're afraid that telling them something negative will hurt their feelings, as they take it personally, which turns into a full-blown fight. You think that it's better to just leave your opinions to yourself, so you can avoid conflict altogether. However, if you really care about this person, you'll be honest with them. Using constructive criticism can help you to be open and honest in a respectful way. In this example you can see how to provide constructive criticism when you think someone could improve at something.

Colleague: *How did you like my presentation yesterday?*

You: *You did a good job considering the requirements, but I feel like there were a few ways you can improve your* presentation before you do it in front of the big bosses. Would you mind if I gave you some tips?

Colleague: Yeah sure. I guess there's always room for improvement.

You: I just want to help you, so you can get the positive recognition you deserve as an employee in this company. Firstly, I think if you compare our products to our competitors,' you should do it in a way that shows we are better than them.

Colleague: You're right. The boss probably wouldn't like me insulting our business. Do you have any other tips?

You: When you present your pitch, you must leave those notecards behind. When you're constantly reading them out loud, it makes it look like you aren't confident in what you're saying. Try to memorize what you most need to say, and free-style the rest. This will make your presentation sound more convincing and enjoyable!

Colleague: *Thank you. I usually don't like being told when I've done something wrong because I'm a perfectionist, but that constructive criticism is actually valuable and I'll use it for the presentation next week.*

Instead of just telling your colleague that their presentation is not good enough, you used constructive criticism to help them approve. If you just listed the amount of things that were wrong with the presentation, you could have hurt their feelings, and started conflict. But if you kept your opinions to yourself when they asked, they would've done badly in their presentation. Providing them with constructive criticism was the perfect sweet spot, as you not only told them what could be better, but you also explained how they can make it better. People are less likely to take offense at criticism when they can see it's coming from a place of helpfulness and care.

Example 2 - Setting Boundaries

Learning how to set boundaries in your relationships is important, no matter how close you are to the person. For every relationship in your life, you need to have boundaries, so you can respect each other and communicate effectively. You may find that people you're really close to in your life say and do things that make you feel uncomfortable, but you don't know how to tell them this. Being able to set healthy boundaries is important for your relationships to prosper, and to avoid conflict in the future. This example shows you how to set boundaries in a healthy and respectful manner, without offending anyone.

Sister: *I told mom about your date with that new guy. She said that you need to find yourself a nice guy already.*

You: *I'm really happy that you have a healthy and open relationship with mom, but I don't unfortunately. Mom judges me for everything that I do, especially when it comes to relationships. That's why I don't tell her about my personal life anymore, so I'd really appreciate it if you keep what*

I tell you between us. I talk to you about my life because you're a safe space, and I really don't feel like being judged or scrutinized by mom. Do you get what I mean?

Sister: *Oh gosh, I'm so sorry I told her. I thought you wouldn't mind, since you know mom and I talk about everything. But don't worry, I understand what you mean, and I'll never tell her about your personal life again.*

You: *Thank you so much for understanding. Also, if there's anything you don't like me doing, please feel free to tell me as well, okay?*

Sister: *I definitely will, but you're the perfect sister so I have no complaints.*

This example shows you how you can ask for boundaries in a relationship without making the other person feel like they're being attacked or blamed. You spoke about the situation you don't like, and explained why it made you uncomfortable, instead of just blaming your sister. At the end of the conversation, you even gave your sister the opportunity to open up about their own feelings and need for boundaries, which shows you're able to respect other people's boundaries and feelings.

Example 3 - Resolving Conflict Together

Resolving conflict between two people isn't a one-man sport. You need to be able to work with the other person to resolve the conflict between you. Although the other individual may not seem interested in conflict resolution, you can influence it by being the bigger person. Sometimes you need to apologize first and take accountability, to set the tone for the resolution. In this example, you can see how you can initiate conflict resolution.

You: *I think we really need to talk about what happened yesterday now that we've calmed down a bit.*

Friend: I agree, but where do we even start? I'm still feeling really upset about the way you spoke to me.

You: I'm really sorry for how I treated you, you didn't deserve that at all. I don't know why I got so upset and started saying hurtful things to you, but I really didn't mean what I said.

Friend: I really appreciate you taking accountability for your actions and words.

You: I'm also hurt by what you said to me. Although I was wrong for what I did, you didn't have to say such hurtful things to me.

Friend: Yes, you're right. I'm so sorry for how I retaliated, it was very uncalled for and I realize that now.

You: I forgive you, but how do we stop this from occurring again in the future, because I hate it when we fight. We both care about each other, so why do we have unnecessary fights that leave both of us upset at the end of the day?

Friend: *I agree with you, because these fights don't even need to happen. I know I would get less upset and angry if you didn't compare me to your other friends, because that really triggers me emotionally.*

You: *I understand what you're saying. I won't do that to you again!*

This example shows you how you can resolve conflict with a simple conversation, however, this conversation may be more intense, in-depth, or longer, depending on the situation. Being able to admit where you went wrong first helps this conversation to go a lot smoother, as the other person doesn't have to be so defensive and angry. It was also valuable and effective to end the conversation by considering what your steps forward should be, so you can avoid experiencing conflict like this again.

CHAPTER 9

Empathetic Communication

"Emotional awareness is necessary so you can properly convey your thoughts and feelings to the other person." – Jason Goldberg

To be a healthy and effective communicator, you need to be able to communicate with empathy. This means that you use your words and communication skills to show your genuine care for the person you're communicating with. When you use empathy while communicating, you're more likely to create emotional connections. If you're trying to be an empathetic communicator, you need to learn how to be a better listener.

Communicating With Empathy

When you talk to the people in your life, how do you communicate with them? Do you talk and listen with empathy, or do you talk mainly considering yourself? It's valuable to consider what your motives are when communicating, as you may find that you're more focused on yourself than you realized. You need to make your conversations and communication more about caring about others, so you can build connections and improve your relationships.

The Art of Being More Empathetic

You may be thinking to yourself that you're an empathetic person, but many of us fail to show our empathy for others through communication. Although you may be thinking with empathy, are you manifesting it, and showing it to the people you communicate with? You can use the following steps to help you to be a more empathetic individual:

1. **Listen first.** Before you communicate anything with empathy, you need to first be able to listen attentively to what the other person has to say. You want to respond in a way that makes the other person feel heard and understood, which requires you to take a close listen to what they have to say. Don't interrupt what they're saying, as this will make them feel unheard.
2. **Put yourself in their shoes.** When you listen to the people around you, you shouldn't space out and think about yourself, as you need to be actively thinking about what they're expressing to you. A great way to help you be more empathetic toward them, is by putting yourself in their shoes. Listen to what they're telling you, and imagine what you'd feel like if you were in their position. Doing this helps you to channel the negative

emotions they're experiencing, which can help you to be a lot sensitive toward their needs.
3. **Talk about them.** Lastly, when you start to respond to them, you must make sure the focus of the conversation is on them. Many people like to communicate about something challenging by bringing up their own experience or sob story. Although it may be nice for the other person to feel like they're not alone, don't steal the spotlight from them. Think about how they're feeling, and say something that will make them feel heard.

Creating Emotional Connections With Empathy

If you're looking to create emotional connections in your life, you need to be able to show your empathetic and sensitive side when you communicate with others. You need to show people that you do care about them and their feelings. This will make it easier for them to get closer to you, as well as make them more likely to open up to you.

Showing empathy by listening to others, giving them advice, and giving them a chance to be vulnerable will ultimately show people that you're a good person to have around. This will make people want to be around you and have you in their lives, as they trust you and feel comfortable around you.

The Power of Expressing Gratitude and Appreciation

When you're building emotional connections with empathy, you need to be able to express gratitude and appreciation. Being empathetic is not just about being there when things are rough, as you need to make the people in your life feel good about themselves by showering them with gratitude and appreciation every now and then. We often take the people in our lives for granted, so it's important to express gratitude and appreciation when you can.

You can simply achieve this by saying kind words every now and then. Let them know how appreciated they are, by telling them you love them when you can, and giving them valuable compliments. You can also show people how grateful you are for them through kind gestures. Make them their favorite meal, engage in fun activities, and take them to their favorite place. Doing kind things for the people you love shows them that they're loved and appreciated.

Examples of Expressing Empathetic Communication

If you're struggling to put your empathetic skills into practice, it's valuable to see examples of how you can achieve empathy through your dialogue. If you're a less emotional or empathetic person, you may struggle to say the right things in the moment. You don't know when is the right time to express and show love and comfort, and you're also unsure of what to say that's appropriate. Learning examples of how you can be empathetic in different real life scenarios can help you practice empathy in your everyday life.

Example 1 - Friend Going Through a Hard Time

In this example, you can see how you can comfort a friend who is going through something challenging in their lives. Unfortunately, the people in our lives will always go through challenging experience, because life isn't simple. Being a great support system for the people in your life by communicating with empathy will strengthen your relationship with them, as well as they will treat you with the same care when you find yourself in a rough situation in life. Through this dialogue you can see how to be that support system to someone in yout life going through challenging experiences.

Friend: I can't believe that just happened…

You: What happened? Are you okay?

Friend: I just lost my job, and I don't know what I'm going to do. I have so much to pay for, I can't afford to be unemployed right now, even for a month!

You: I'm so sorry to hear that. I can imagine how stressed you are right now, but just know that I'm here for you. Unfortunately, I don't have a lot of money to lend to you, but I will help you as much as I can. I'll help you to job hunt, and you'll get back on your feet in no time. I believe in you, and I'm here for you!

Friend: Thank you so much. Just having your support means so much to me.

This is a perfect example of how you can comfort someone you're close to. Your friend is going through a distressing situation, and instead of judging or invalidating their experience, you fully comfort them in their time of need. This helps them to feel better about the situation, as they know you're there to support them emotionally. Although you don't have the money to support them financially, you communicated how you will be there for them in every way you can.

Example 2 - Someone Trying to Open Up

In this example, you can see how to give someone the space and time to open up, by using empathy when you're communicating. If someone in your life is trying to open up to you, it's your job to simply listen to them. You may be used to always having a response, but sometimes it's important to just listen attentively. In this dialogue you can see how you must be a good listener who shows care and empathy.

You: How was your day, love?

Partner: You will not believe the day I had. It felt like the universe was just against me today… But you don't want to hear me drone on about my day, so don't worry.

You: Of course I want to hear about your day! I care about you, and I want to know what happened, so I can be there for you.

Partner: I really appreciate that, babe. Well, where do I even start? I know it may sound silly, but I knew my day was going to suck when it started off with me spilling all of my coffee on myself. Then when I got to work my boss had ten million complaints for me as soon as I walked into the door. It was like everyone had a problem with me today, and it was so frustrating. And on top of that I had to work extra hours, and all I wanted to do was come home. It just wasn't my day today. Thank you for listening to me. I really needed to get all of that off my chest.

You: *Of course, love. I will always be here for you if you need to vent. I'm really sorry your day was like that, but let's have a good evening together to make up for it.*

Being able to comfort your partner or loved one when they're having a bad day is so important. You want to be able to show empathy by making sure the people you care about know you're there to hear them vent, or get something off their chest. Although you may not have the advice or the facilities to make all of their problems go away, simply listening to them with compassion shows your empathy and care toward them.

Practicing Listening Skills

If you want to be an empathetic communicator, it's crucial to practice listening skills. You can't be seen as empathetic and caring if you don't truly listen to what other people have to say. Although you may think that you are a good listener, you may not be hearing other people out the way they want to be heard. You need to truly hear and understand what people are saying to you, in order to respond with empathy and sincerity.

The 3 A's of Active Listening

Before learning how you can be a better listener, you may want to consider the 3 A's of active listening. These three A's—attitude, attention, adjustment—can be valuable as they help you to check yourself when you're communicating with someone. Consider if you're portraying these three A's, and if you're not you should discover how to improve your listening in that moment. Here is how you can utilize the 3 A's when listening:

1. **Attitude.** Your attitude when listening to people makes an impact on how well you listen. When you feel negative and fed up, you're less

likely to take in what other people are saying. You need to have a positive attitude to listen attentively.

2. **Attention.** Many people don't have good attention spans, but you need to train yourself to pay attention to what others are saying. You need to stay focused and engaged, as well as show the other person that you are listening, through your responses and body language.

3. **Adjustment.** When listening to someone, you may be thinking with your own solid opinions, which can make you close-minded to what they have to say. You must be able to adjust your mindset, to fully understand what the other person has to say.

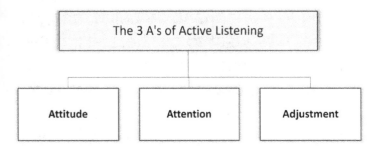

How to Be a Better Listener

Being a better listener is all about **leaving your own personal agenda behind**, so you can focus solely on what the other person is saying to you. You may have come into the conversation with the intention of bringing something up, or talking about yourself, but it turned into a conversation about the other person. Instead of cutting them off and resuming to talk about yourself, you need to leave your agenda behind, and give this person their moment, as your moment will come as well.

You also need to **listen with the objective of learning**. If you're just listening to someone to be polite, and you don't actually want to be there, it'll reflect in your responses and body language. You need to show genuine interest in the person you're listening to, by genuinely trying to understand what they're saying. When you do this you may find that you learn a lot about their situation, and them as individuals.

This can be achieved in a couple ways. You can **ask them questions to show your interest**, but don't bombard them with so many questions that it feels like an interrogation. When you ask questions related to what they're talking about, it shows that you're listening, as well as prove to them that you're interested in what they have to say.

The most important way to show that you're listening to someone else is by **preventing yourself from interrupting**. You may have something you want to say about what they're currently talking about, but wait to share your thoughts until you can see they're done with their own thoughts. You can also show your attentiveness by repeating back to them what they're saying, and nodding your head frequently. Although this may sound silly, it does show the other person that you're hearing what they're saying.

What Not to Do

You may think that you're an excellent listener, but you're unaware of the fact that other people don't feel like they're being attentively listened to. It's important to know what not to do when you're trying to communicate with empathy. This is an example of a dialogue that shows you what not to do when you're listening to people with empathy.

Sister: I'm so annoyed with my friend. She's always trying to belittle me, and make me feel as though I'm less important or intelligent than she is.

You: Oh my gosh, I hate people like that. I have a friend who does the exact same thing and it always makes me feel worthless, and like she thinks she's better than me. Unfortunately, I work with her so I can't avoid her.

Sister: Well, I'm not sure what to do in my situation. I love her a lot because she's a close friend of mine, but I'm really tired of being made to feel so small.

You: In my situation I just avoid my colleague at all costs. Literally any confrontation with them annoys me.

Sister: I think I will…

You: And I just remembered why she does that to me! I remember my other colleague, who I actually like, told me that she treats me like that because she is jealous of me.

After reading that dialogue, what do you think is wrong with it? Being able to determine what's wrong with this conversation can help you be aware of what to avoid when you're trying to be an attentive and empathetic communicator. In this conversation, you can see all the different ways you communicated in the wrong way. It's important to recognize these types of bad communication habits, as it can be easy to slip up with them.

Let's take a look at some of the things that went wrong on your side in the conversation example. Firstly, when your sister was opening up to you about something they were struggling with, you turned the conversation to yourself, by explaining how you struggled with the same thing. This took all of the attention off them, as you made the situation about yourself.

You may think you're showing empathy by relating to what the other person has to say, but instead you're doing the opposite, by making the situation about you. On top of that, you don't give the other person the space to talk about what they're going through, as you continuously interrupt them, and what they're trying to say. This makes them feel even more unheard and neglected at the moment.

Steps to Be a Better Listener

If you follow the previous tips, and you find yourself struggling to become a better listener, then these following steps will help you. In the moment when you're talking to other people, you find yourself struggling to focus and listen to what the other person has to say. When you find yourself in this dilemma, it's valuable to use the following steps, as they keep you on track to listen effectively:

1. **Be observant of the talking ratio.** The first thing you must do is consider what the listening to talking ratio is. If you notice that you're talking more than the other person, it's important for you to keep quiet, and provide the other person with space to speak. You need to stop yourself from interrupting them, and realize not every conversation topic needs to be about you. Although it's not nice to come to terms with, sometimes listening is more valuable than talking about yourself.
2. **Ask them effective questions.** If you feel like you were talking too much, and this has caused the other

person to become more reserved, it's time for you to ask questions to help encourage their talking. By asking them questions, you're essentially letting them know that it's their time to shine. You're giving them the opportunity to continue talking about what they wanted to talk about, and your questions show your genuine interest in what they have to say to you.

3. **Show your care.** If you've been failing at listening to someone attentively, then you want to make an effort to show that you actually care about what they have to say to you. You can do this by improving your body language, by making it more open and caring. Using the right vocabulary that shows thoughtfulness and care also helps the other person realize that you're listening attentively, with care. When you show empathy and listening skills through your communication, the other person will forgive you for dismissing them previously.

We all get used to our communication habits, which can cause us to practice toxic communication tactics that make us disregard other people's words. Although you may not think you're guilty of this, it could be an unhealthy habit you've adapted over time. The most important thing is being able to identify when you're being a bad listener, and insensitive to other people's feelings, so you can implement the previous steps.

CHAPTER 10

Powerful Speakers Can Change the World

"Communication is one of the most important skills you require for a successful life." – Catherine Pulsifer

We all get so used to our communication habits that we get comfortable in our conversation habits and ineffective communication techniques. If you want to reach greater heights in your life, practicing effective communication can be at the root of it all. With effective communication, you can build new relationships, and improve broken ones. You can build emotional connections that bring genuine love and happiness into your life.

Effective communication isn't just for building relationships, but it can also help you to get further in your career. If you want to find success, get your dream job, or be happier in your workplace, you can use all of the communication techniques discussed above to make a better world for yourself. You can even consider thinking bigger, by considering how your powerful communication skills can positively influence the world around you. You actually have the power to make a difference and influence others through effective and valuable communication.

You may not realize it, but your words have a bigger impact on others than you may realize. Think about a time someone said something nasty to you, and it ruined your mood that day. Then, consider a compliment you got from someone and how it made you feel so good about yourself that day. You too have the power to change someone's day with the power of your words, so it's your choice to be a good or bad mood changer in someone's day.

Trying to advance in the work environment can be tricky, especially when you have to do speeches and presentations frequently. You feel overwhelmed and afraid when you're required to do any kind of public speaking, and when you do it you find yourself fumbling on your words, and not performing to the best of your ability. There's one colleague who always presents speeches flawlessly, and they get all the praise. Just for one moment, you want to be in the limelight and get the same recognition. You can be the person everyone looks up to by using effective communication skills. Learning how to deliver speeches with confidence, and practicing how to keep your composure even when you're asked questions, will help you to be the person about whom everyone asks, "How do they do it?"

You will find that you find more success in your career, as people begin to respect you. How you communicate to people has an impact on how much they respect you. If you're passive, people will walk over you, and they will never take you seriously. However, if you communicate with aggression or passive aggression, people won't want to be around you. When you are assertive and confident whenever you communicate to your colleagues or bosses, they will start to recognize how valuable you are.

It's mind blowing to realize that you have the power to influence what people do, how they perceive you, and whether they want to form an emotional bond with you, all through effective and powerful communication. You can control your reality, as well as the reality of the people around you, by choosing your words wisely, using welcoming body language, knowing when to keep quiet and listen, and asking and answering the right questions. When you put all of these tips and techniques together in your everyday life and the conversations you experience, you will be a force to be reckoned with.

Conclusion

Congratulations, you've finished reading a book that is going to help you to transform your communication, and improve your life drastically! Reading this book was the first step to becoming an effective and confident communicator who attracts and influences people around them. Now it's time for you to take the tips and techniques from this book, and apply them to your daily conversations and communication.

The words you use, how you say them, when you say them, and how you use your body language when saying them, all have an impact on how effective your communication is. You need to holistically consider how you communicate with others, so that you can ensure that you communicate with confidence, **assertion**, empathy, and self-awareness.

When you do this, you will be able to handle any situation with your communication skills, whether it's a matter of conflict, or you're nervous to make a positive first impression, or you don't know how to build an emotional connection. Whatever the issue or situation is, you can use your effective communication to tackle it, and impress the person you're communicating with.

You wake up next to your partner who serves you delicious breakfast in bed to show you appreciation for how empathetic and loving you are toward them. You get ready and go to work, and everyone greets you as you walk past them. You get into your new office, as you received a big promotion for delivering the best pitch that scored an amazing deal for the company.

Throughout your day at work, you bring forward ideas, and everyone listens to you and loves what you actually have to say. You make real changes in your office and your company that are for the greater good of everyone. Not only do you live a better, more fulfilling life because of your exceptional communication skills, but you also inspire people around you. They see how you walk and talk with confidence, and this motivates them to also communicate with assertion and confidence.

If you practice the effective communication tools that have been provided to you throughout this book, this success story can become your reality. You can live this reality, or any reality that you desire, by using the right communication to impact the people around you. However, this change won't occur if you don't take the time to practice effective communication. You may not be the best communicator at first, but with time and practice, you will find yourself being a naturally assertive and confident communicator whom everyone admires and respects.

CPSIA information can be obtained
at www.ICGtesting.com
Printed in the USA
LVHW051813010723
751014LV00010B/206